TALKING POINT

ANIMALS BEHIND BARS

Sylvia

Cover illustration by
Mark Thomas

SCHOLASTIC

Scholastic Children's Books,
Commonwealth House, 1-19 New Oxford Street,
London WC1A 1NU, UK
A division of Scholastic Ltd
London ~ New York ~ Toronto ~ Sydney ~ Auckland
Mexico City ~ New Delhi ~ Hong Kong

Published in the UK by Scholastic Ltd, 1999

ISBN 0 590 19813 0

Typeset by Rapid Reprographics Ltd
Printed by Cox & Wyman Ltd, Reading, Berks.

10 9 8 7 6 5 4 3 2 1

CONTENTS

INTRODUCTION

Sabina is 14 years old and suffers from Cystic Fibrosis, or CF. You can abbreviate the name of the disease but you can't lessen the impact it has on her life. The disease causes chronic infection in Sabina's lungs and every day they fill up with sticky fluid. If she doesn't have lung therapy several times a day, she will drown in the fluids produced by her own body.

Sabina is pinning her hopes on a mouse that has been genetically altered so that it carries the same gene defect found in most CF sufferers. CF mice are being used to study how the disease operates and to test new drugs. With luck, they will help speed up the discovery of a cure for this deadly disease. Sabina is hoping it will come sooner rather than later.

The mice that might mean the difference between life and death for Sabina, and thousands of young people like her, are paying a high price for our sake. And they're not alone. Several years ago, people woke up to the fact that certain kinds of entertainment, the food most of us eat and the things we buy to make ourselves look good or feel better all come with an additional price tag that money can't even begin to touch. And it's a price paid strictly by animals. This book is about those animals.

For years, we locked animals behind bars in zoos, in factory farms and in research laboratories without so much as a second thought. Then animal rights groups and writers like Peter Singer and Marian Stamp Dawkin drew our attention to what happens to animals inside these institutions. And we began to ask ourselves some tough questions. Do animals suffer from being captive, or are they so unlike us they don't care? Do we have any right to treat animals the way we do? Should we shut down all zoos, factory farms and animal research laboratories? Or should animal rights groups shut up shop instead and stop trying to make us feel guilty about something as essential as the conservation of endangered species or the production of food and medicine?

Few people are willing to see the world in such black and white terms. A reality check suggests that the path to walk is in varying shades of grey. But how do you find that path when you're dealing with such emotionally loaded issues? You have to balance gut-level feelings against rational thought, but it's particularly difficult to do when the issue becomes personal.

For instance, as a teenager, you're more at risk from meningitis than older people are. The very word meningitis can strike terror into the heart of a community. It's a highly infectious disease caused by several types of bacteria or viruses, and it swells the covering of the brain and spinal cord. There isn't a year goes by without one or more outbreaks in a school, college or university. You might even know someone who's been struck down by meningitis. During the 1995 outbreak in the UK alone there were 200 deaths.

Research on mice and rabbits has helped to develop a vaccine against one type of meningitis. The result is that Hib meningitis is now very rare in the UK. Why should we stop doing animal research if it provides the best hope of finding vaccines for other strains of the disease? Isn't your life worth more than that of a mouse or a rabbit? That, of course, is the gut-level reaction that most people would have to such an emotional issue. The more measured, rational reaction usually comes later.

Are there, for instance, any other ways of finding more vaccines without using animals? And if it's discovered that we can get close to a solution using non-animal research but there's one crucial step that must be tested on animals, can we find a way of doing it so that they don't suffer? If we can do all that, are we then morally justified in sacrificing the mouse or rabbit for the human – or to save the lives of fellow animals?

There's nothing wrong with feeling passionately about something. Many people give up eating meat simply because they can't stand to think of themselves as the cause of animal suffering. But you can't begin to make truly rational decisions about issues until you're sure of your facts. How do you sort out those facts? Zoologists and researchers claim one thing, animal rights and welfare groups claim another. Who do you believe?

This book attempts to assemble the main arguments for and against what we do to animals in zoos, factory farms and research laboratories. Scattered amongst all those facts are many thought-provoking questions and explanations, as well as claims and observations by the people involved. You'll find many opposing points of view in its pages but few conclusions – you must come to those yourself. Just remember that everyone involved in such emotional issues sees things from their own perspective, which isn't necessarily the only one that's valid.

And finally, you'll find a sting in the tail of this book. The last chapter asks some of the toughest questions of all. How do we know whether animals suffer in captivity or whether they're aware of themselves and what we do to them? Can they feel emotions like we do? Do we treat pets in our own homes any better than we treat wild animals in zoos or domesticated animals in factory farms or laboratories? On that note, why don't you snuggle up with the family pet (or, if you don't have one, how about your best mate?) and prepare to prise apart a few iron bars and set free some mind-blowing animal facts?

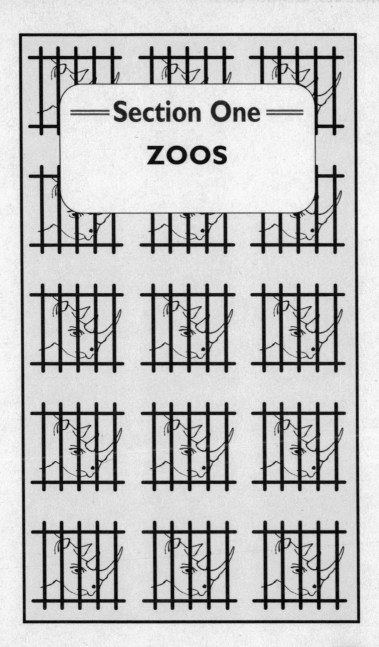

Section One

ZOOS

'The good zoos of the world can be counted on the fingers of one thumb.'
Gerald Durrell, zoologist, 1994

In 1947, a male gorilla arrived at London Zoo. He was named Guy and he spent the next 30 years in what amounts to solitary confinement. Of course, our attitudes towards animals were different back then. Guy was a huge attraction at the zoo. And it's unlikely that many visitors questioned whether we were wrong to lock him up for the rest of his life without companions or a mate. By the time an African elephant named Pole Pole (pronounced Poly Poly) had to be put down by lethal injection at the same zoo in 1983, however, we had been sitting up and taking notice for some time. It's hardly surprising then that, several years later, when animal rights groups and the media focused on the incessant pacing of a polar bear named Misha at Bristol Zoo Gardens, we were ready to believe that zoos were in the business of driving animals mad.

If you're thinking that British zoos sound as if they're among the worst in the world, you're wrong. There are some truly excellent zoos in the world, as well as many zoos that need to work harder for their animals, and far too many zoos that are so bad they should be closed down. British zoos can be slotted into the first two categories. The Zoo Licensing Act of 1981 acknowledges that we have a duty towards animals by setting minimum standards for zoos in this country.

In many other parts of the world, even these minimum standards aren't required by law. When duty can't be enforced by law, anything can and does happen. Animals in Kuwait Zoo were used for target practice by Iraqi forces in the aftermath of the Gulf War. And the only thing that prevented animals at the cash-strapped Tbilisi Zoo in

Georgia from starving to death was the timely appearance of an animal welfare rescue team. Check out some back issues of newspapers at your local library and you won't have to look long before you find stories of the misery of animals in one zoo or another.

❑ The zoo squad
In Britain, the Secretary of State for the Environment specifies the minimum standards for zoos, as set out in the Zoo Licensing Act of 1981. Under the Act, local authorities have the power to inspect British zoos and close down any that don't meet the standards. The majority of the world's zoos are under no legal requirement to comply with any standards of animal welfare, minimal or otherwise.

Many of us have a love/hate relationship with zoos. We love the idea of being able to see exotic animals in the flesh as much as we hate the idea of locking them up. Of course, you can argue that animals don't understand our concept of freedom. Most wild animals, with the exception of those that migrate long distances, live their entire lives without stepping outside their limited home range. They haven't the slightest inclination to go walkabout just to see what the scenery's like over the next hill. So does it really matter to them where they live as long as they have plenty of food and are free from danger? Are we being hopelessly sentimental in the way we think about zoo animals, or worse – callous and close-minded? Do animals suffer in zoos? And is there one good reason why we should continue to keep animals in zoos?

What's your opinion?

Before you read any further, put your current beliefs about zoos on record by deciding whether you agree with these statements or not. If you can't make up your mind, don't worry – just tick the 'Don't know' box. You'll have more opportunities to make a decision before you finish the book.

Zoos make animals suffer.

Sounds right to me. ☐

Sounds like rubbish. ☐

Maybe not all animals. ☐

Don't know. ☐

Zoos used to be strictly for entertainment. Now they're more concerned with education and conservation.

Sounds right to me. ☐

Sounds like rubbish. ☐

Maybe some zoos are. ☐

Don't know. ☐

Zoos can help to save endangered species.

Sounds right to me. ☐

Sounds like rubbish. ☐

Maybe some zoos can. ☐

Don't know. ☐

Zoos should be shut down.

Sounds right to me. ☐

Sounds like rubbish. ☐

Maybe some zoos should be. ☐

Don't know. ☐

What zoo supporters say:
- You can say goodbye to many large animals by 2020 unless we use zoos to help save them.
- Zoos prod people into taking action to save animals and their wild homes.
- Which is worse: letting a species die out or breeding it in a zoo?
- Without zoos, animals like the Arabian oryx would no longer be living in the wild.
- It's rubbish to claim that all animals suffer in zoos. Some thrive in them.
- Zoo staff have the know-how and experience that conservationists need.

What anti-zoo campaigners say:
- Animals go mad in zoos.
- Zoos are for the benefit of people, not animals.
- Zoos destroy animals they don't need, or sell them to laboratories or circuses.
- Zoos do little for conservation. The vast majority of animals bred in zoos are not endangered.
- We have no right to imprison animals for our own pleasure.

DO ANIMALS SUFFER IN ZOOS?

'There are possibly 10,000 zoos around the world containing between 2 and 5 million animals... In the majority of cases, little or sometimes no recognition is made of the animals' welfare needs.'
Will Travers, Director, Born Free Foundation

First ask yourself why there are so many zoos, not only in Britain but all around the world. Until recently, people never seemed to question whether it was wrong to imprison animals for our own pleasure. Maybe it's because if you do something long enough it becomes the accepted thing, the traditional thing, to do regardless of whether it's right or wrong. And zoos certainly have a long tradition. We've been locking up animals in parks and private menageries for about 4,500 years. (Just after we learned how to chisel messages to each other on stone tablets.)

The ancient Egyptians, for instance, captured bulls, snakes, hippos, owls, crocodiles and scarab beetles in the belief that they were sacred beings. Egyptian priests might have known how to keep their gods happy, but they knew next to nothing about keeping animals happy in their temples. The mummified remains of these sacred animals show evidence of bone deformity and neglect. Other animals were kept as status symbols by the pharaohs. One even took his pet lion into battle with him. There wasn't a ruler worth his or her salt in the ancient world who didn't have a private animal collection as a symbol of wealth and power.

Wild animal collections remained the exclusive property of the rich and famous for thousands of years, until Alexander the Great installed what was probably the world's first public zoo in the port of Alexandria in Egypt. A trip to the zoo quickly became everyone's idea of fun from Constantinople to ancient Rome.

Over the centuries, zoo designers have all had to solve the same problem – how to create a zoo that takes care of its animals' needs, makes the keeper's job as safe as possible and gives the audience a terrific view. Not an easy job, since all three have opposing needs. Different styles of zoos have solved the problem – in different ways. Animal parks, in which tamed cheetahs and lions roamed free, were favourites of ancient Egyptian kings and were undoubtedly harder on the keepers than the animals. But it's safe to say that throughout history, both the audience and the keepers usually had a much more rewarding time than the animals.

By Victorian times the idea was to catch as many different types of exotic animals as possible – the more the better because many of them didn't survive for long – and display them, one to a cage, like freaks in a sideshow. Today, we call them 'postage stamp' zoos. Zoo design has changed dramatically since these cruel Victorian menageries, coming down more on the side of the animals.

What do you think?
Just because it's now possible, thanks to improved vet care and nutrition, to keep an animal physically healthy in captivity for many years, while it produces offspring and lives in an enclosure that looks pleasing to us, does it follow that the animal is happy?

'Going mad behind bars'

►This headline appeared on an article in the *Mail on Sunday* on 20 March, 1994 – one of several newspaper features on the impact of captivity on zoo animals. Who was going mad behind bars? Supposedly, the polar bear Misha, whom you met on page 13. Misha, who died two years before the article was published, had lived at Bristol Zoo Gardens with his mate Nina since 1979. What attracted the attention of animal support groups was his pacing. Back and forth he went, the same number of steps forward and back, over and over again.

This kind of restless, repetitive, meaningless action is found in zoos, on farms, in research laboratories, in kennels – wherever animals are denied the opportunity to get on with their lives in their own way. Scientists call it stereotypic behaviour. (A very clinical, unemotional name for something that has fired plenty of emotional response from humans.) Some think it's a sign of frustration and stress, even madness. Others disagree and claim it could just as easily be something as trivial as a harmless way of passing the time. In other words, no one can claim with certainty to know what causes it. Scientists might not agree on the cause of Misha's pacing, but the newspapers had no trouble deciding he was barking mad. Soon Bristol Zoo became notorious for driving Misha crazy. Unfortunately, in this instance, someone hadn't done their homework properly.

It appears that Bristol Zoo rescued Misha in 1979 from a circus (the real villain in the story), where he had spent most of his time in a so-called 'beast wagon'. The few steps forward and back that Misha traced out over and over again in his enclosure at the zoo matched the dimensions of his cramped circus wagon. No matter how much space the zoo gave Misha, he seemed bound by the invisible bars of his former prison. A spokesperson for the zoo insists that Misha usually only paced when visitors were present. Even so, the zoo tried to help him break his pacing habit by bringing in an animal psychologist who studied both Misha and his mate and suggested ways to improve their lives. You're probably not surprised to discover that when Misha had interesting toys to play with, such as barrels, traffic cones and garlic-flavoured logs, and had to work to find his food (sometimes frozen in ice, other times scattered around his enclosure), he spent much less time pacing.

The moral of the story, of course, is that while animal rights groups were right to want to draw attention to Misha's abnormal behaviour because it was a sign that something was wrong, what they and the media failed to recognize was that one aspect of an animal's behaviour doesn't necessarily give an accurate overall picture of how well it's presently being cared for. According to zoo staff, Misha was far from mad, and his pacing hadn't been caused by his zoo environment. On the contrary, the zoo had taken steps to improve the life of both polar bears.

It's worthwhile bearing in mind, however, that the awkward glare of publicity, a direct result of the constant lobbying of animal rights groups, has motivated many zoos to improve the lives of their animals. Whether they would have invested so much effort and money in the behavioural research needed to make this happen without being prodded is anyone's guess. And many zoos in Britain, including Bristol, still have work to do replacing small, inadequate display spaces with enclosures that show genuine concern for the needs of their animals.

❏ Big top surprise

The RSPCA commissioned a respected British scientist to do an independent study on the welfare of animals in 15 British circuses. She concluded that, for the most part, circus animals weren't any worse off than animals in zoos, private stables or kennels. In fact, circus animals might even be happier than zoo animals. Why? Because their days aren't so monotonous.

The scientist found no evidence of cruelty during the training sessions she was invited to watch, and no evidence of distress during transportation as the animals seemed to become used to it. She did, however, find much to complain about in the welfare of the animals when they weren't travelling or performing. Even so, she observed no more stereotypic behaviours in circus animals than in zoo or farm animals.

Although the RSPCA did not publish the findings of this report, many circuses took notice of the scientist's recommendations and have provided exercise yards for use by big animals when they're not travelling or performing so that they can leave their beast wagons from time to time. She also recommended more training in the belief that animals would benefit from the challenge of having to learn new things. The scientist decided that the arguments that circuses cause suffering and distress to animals and that making animals perform tricks for our entertainment undermines our respect for them – were invalid. What do you think?

> **Believe it or not!**
> If you ever see a male panda doing a handstand with his belly to the wall, you'll know he's marking the wall as his territory.

What causes 'zoo madness'?

➤Unless you've been abroad, you've probably never visited a 'postage stamp' zoo – the kind that contains one iron-barred, concrete box after another with one or two stressed-out, bored animals on display in each box. No better than the Victorian menagerie. The kind one newspaper describes as a 'cruel zoo' and which the vet who inspects British zoos for the Department of the Environment decribes as providing 'a life sentence in a concrete box' for its inhabitants. It offers no space for the animals. No opportunity for them to escape from the prying eyes of visitors, or to act naturally, let alone have a social life. Living like this every day places great psychological stress on animals. No wonder they end up doing strange things.

Take pacing for instance. All animals have what's called a 'flight distance'. Any stranger that steps inside this comfort zone becomes a threat. The natural reaction to this threat is to run away, and so restore the flight distance to normal. Allowing zoo visitors to get too close to animals that can't run away, therefore, is a form of torture. When the polar bear Misha first experienced this invasion of his comfort zone, his natural reaction would have been to run away. But how far could he run? Only to the walls of his circus wagon. And so he would start to pace back and forth.

At first an animal in a situation like Misha's might only

pace when visitors were present, but as it was offered no relief from stress, it might begin to spend more time pacing and less time doing other things. Eventually, pacing might become the way the animal deals with all kinds of frustrations, such as feeling hungry, not being able to make a nest, or seeing something that whets its appetite and not being able to hunt it.

Over time, a tiring action such as pacing might simplify down into small, bizarre movements. The pace and turn pattern across the back of the cage, for example, might become an odd, repeated twisting of the neck. The more bizarre the behaviour, the worse it is, which means that neck twisting is several steps up the abnormality ladder from pacing. Researchers think that just as humans might chant a mantra – a word or a sound – over and over again to help them block out information from the outside so they can relax and meditate, animals might repeat the same movements as a kind of physical mantra to make themselves feel better. The repetitive movements probably help focus the animal's attention inward on the actions of its body, which has the effect of blotting out its surroundings.

> **Would you suffer if you were locked up indefinitely in a barren cell with no say in what, when or how you eat, with nothing to do all day to ease the boredom and with no chance of making contact with any other human being? Of course you would. Is it feasible then that an animal would suffer under similar conditions?**

Sometimes, however, stereotypic behaviour can go over the top and the animal ends up injuring itself. If an animal grooms or licks itself constantly it can develop open sores that become infected. Some animals have even been known to bite their own legs or tails. Of course, stereotypic behaviours aren't only found in animals in cruel, old-fashioned zoos. Nor are they confined to wild animals. Horses fastened up in stables for much of the time develop such stable 'vices' as cribbing or weaving, in which the horse chews its stable or sways from side to side. Pigs in factory farms bite the bars of their pens or each other's tails. Veal calves confined to crates suck each other's tongues. In fact, most of the research on stereotypic behaviour has been done with farm animals. Even pets have been known to develop quirky behaviours. Dogs locked away for six months in the solitary confinement of quarantine sometimes lick or gnaw compulsively on their own feet until they are raw and bloody.

Is there a cure for 'zoo madness'?

➤When pacing or bar chewing becomes such a habit that the animal only stops doing it while it's asleep or feeding, it's difficult to cure. Researchers have removed what they think are the causes of stereotypic behaviour and improved the life of many zoo animals, such as Misha, yet still the animals pace, sway or lick themselves raw.

There seems to be real hope, however, of helping animals whose abnormal behaviours aren't too pronounced. For instance, a gorilla that only over-grooms before feeding time might be broken of the habit by changing the way it's fed. It's not natural for gorillas to feed only once or twice a day out of a bowl. In the wild, they spend most of their time browsing for food. By covering the floor of the gorilla enclosure with straw and leaves, then scattering food among them so that the animal has to search for it, the zoo creates a feeding situation that feels natural to the gorilla and which fills most of its day with pleasant, meaningful activity. When the gorilla's frustration over not being able to search for its own food is removed, its stereotypic behaviour often disappears.

> **Why shouldn't mammals, whose brains contain the same emotion control area that yours does, feel emotions as you do?**

DO ALL ANIMALS SUFFER IN ZOOS?

It must be apparent to you by now that if constant frustration and boredom are forms of suffering, then many of the animals you see in zoos are suffering. Unfortunately, one of the dilemmas facing researchers is that they can never really know for certain how an animal feels, because it cannot speak. As we belong to the animal kingdom, however, and share many physical similarities with other animals, it's not unreasonable to assume that they, like us, are capable of feeling physical pain or comfort. And if they feel similar physical sensations, why not emotional ones too? The least we can do, if we're not certain, is give them the benefit of the doubt. (For more on this, see Section Four.)

Perhaps, though, not all animals find life in a zoo as stress-filled as others. One of Britain's best known zoologists, the late Gerald Durrell (who founded one of the world's finest conservation zoos, the Jersey Wildlife Preservation Trust) pointed out that some animals can live as satisfying a life in a carefully planned zoo environment as they can in the wild – with none of the dangers of the wild. Durrell's argument was that if an animal isn't going to travel far from its home throughout the course of its life, why couldn't it be just as happy living inside a zoo as outside, particularly if the zoo can reproduce its normal living conditions?

> *'Some animals are happier in zoos than others. Big cats, wolves and similar predators enter a deep depression when confined, and it is only to be regretted that the sight is not more distressing to the average visitor than it seems to be.'*
> *Roger Scruton, Animal Rights and Wrongs, 1996*

Of course, it's easier for a zoo to make small animals feel at home than it is for them to meet the needs of big mammals such as polar bears, elephants or killer whales that roam large territories. But little creatures like insects, spiders, frogs, toads, newts, lizards, snakes and small mammals don't have enough box office draw to attract large crowds of paying customers, whereas bears, big cats, elephants, gorillas and other powerful mammals do. Zoos are expensive to operate, so even the best zoos that are seriously involved in conservation work display these box office stars of the animal world to keep the turnstiles clicking over at the gate. (The good news is that fewer zoos are now displaying big mammals that need travelling room.)

What do you think?

When zoos stopped being the private property of the mega-rich and had to make a profit to survive, they discovered that the way to attract the paying public was to display what zoo people call 'charismatic megafauna'. In other words, powerful animals that have the ability to thrill and chill. In 1936 the biggest crowd puller of them all – the once-mythical giant panda – was captured and put on display at the Brookfield Zoo in Chicago. Su-Lin can be credited with triggering the wave of public sentiment that brought an end to the practice of shooting pandas either for sport or for scientific study.

Were we right to lock up Su-Lin in a zoo if her presence there meant saving the lives of many other pandas? Zoo supporters would see Su-Lin's captivity as a necessary means to an end: one animal gives up its freedom in return for the survival of its species.

(Although in this case it hasn't happened – pandas are still on the brink of extinction, due mainly to habitat loss.) Animal rights groups would question our right to keep any animal captive in a zoo, and would look for other ways to prevent pandas from being hunted. This question uncovers a fundamental difference between the way zoos and animal rights groups see animals. They're both fully in favour of the survival of a species, but the latter places greater emphasis on the rights of the individual animal.

The ABCs of zoo design

➤If zoos insist on displaying big, charismatic animals that suffer more in captivity than many smaller creatures, it's reasonable to ask what they're doing to alleviate their suffering. This question should be foremost in every zoo designer's mind. To make sure zoo animals lead as fulfilling a life as possible – and that doesn't mean completely stress-free, because some stress is vital for a healthy existence – zoo designers must have a detailed knowledge of how animals live in the wild.

Just how necessary this knowledge is can be demonstrated by a near-disaster at London Zoo back in the 1930s when the zoo became a pioneer in providing more natural conditions for its animals. The new baboon enclosure looked wonderfully natural. Surely, everyone thought, the baboons will love it. But instead of peace and harmony ruling in the baboon colony, mayhem broke out. What nobody knew then was that baboons have very strict rules governing the numbers of males and females in baboon society. When ignorant humans got the ratio all wrong, there was blood on the floor of the baboon enclosure. Today, everyone knows how many male and female baboons to put together in one enclosure, thanks to the work of zoologists who have studied baboon societies in the wild. London Zoo, in particular, is well known in scientific circles, although not so much in public ones, for the wealth of research it supports both here and abroad.

Only when zoo designers know all about an animal can they begin to meet its needs. They need to know how, when and what it's fed, whether the animal needs to live alone or with its family or other social group, how much contact it should have with a keeper, how much privacy it needs and whether there needs to be a visual barrier between it and other species. They can work out the best size for its enclosure (within reason, of course, since zoos have limited space and money) and the amount of distance needed between the animal and visitors. And when it comes to furnishing the enclosure, the designer needs to know exactly what kind of 'cage furniture' the animal needs. For instance, if the animal lives in the treetops, it will need tree branches – or other climbing apparatus – high in its enclosure.

The best zoos do this kind of research and are trying to take all these things into account to make sure that their animals lead the happiest lives possible. They've discovered that they don't have to perfectly mimic an animal's wild habitat to make it satisfying to the animal. In fact, some zoos that have done this have only ended up creating something that pleases people. Animals take no pleasure, for instance, in trees they're not allowed to use because they'll damage them. It's often much better, from a tree-dweller's point of view, to have some kind of indestructible frame to climb, perhaps a high platform on which to build a nest and a daily supply of fresh branches to strip of their leaves or play with.

> *It's no good releasing perfect physical specimens of zoo-bred animals into the wild if they don't know how to behave. Zoos must find ways to let animals feel and act as if they're in the wild.*

One of the jobs of researchers in zoos is to come up with inexpensive and ingenious ways to enrich the lives of their animals and give them opportunities to act naturally so they don't lose their wild behaviours. They can be as simple as building a platform so that cheetahs can climb on to it, just as they climb on to termite mounds in the wild to gain a clear view of their surroundings. Or to give large plastic containers to polar bears so they can thump on them with their front feet, just as they thump on the ice dens of seals to smash them open. And while it's not practical to give polar bears snow each night to shape into a nest, they're perfectly happy making their nests out of straw.

❏ **It's only natural**

• **Glasgow Zoo reduces pacing among ocelots by feeding four times a day instead of once. Keepers hide the midday feed of chopped meat and raw eggs among the branches of a woodpile so the cats spend the afternoon figuring out how to get at their lunch.**

• **In the wild, an adult lar gibbon couple sing a duet to defend their territory, then a nearby couple respond with their song. The single family of lar gibbons at London Zoo had no neighbouring gibbons they could serenade. So staff broadcast a wild couple's duet twice a day and the zoo gibbons enthusiastically respond.**

- The chimp enclosure at Sydney's Taranoga Zoo might not look much like the natural habitat of chimps in Africa, but it offers them something much more important – the freedom and space to relate to each other as they would in the wild.
- Bears love honey, so Copenhagen Zoo makes sure its bears get their share. At random times throughout the day, honey is pumped into artificial trees. As soon as the bears hear the pump, they climb the trees and spend a sticky hour or two licking their honey-covered paws.
- How do you help predators practise their hunting skills in captivity? Cologne Zoo solved this problem for its hunting dogs by hanging meat from the underbelly of a rubber zebra and whizzing the zebra speedily across their enclosure. The dogs are able to chase the zebra and grab on to the meat using the same tactics as they would in the wild to get their food.

DO WE REALLY NEED ZOOS?

'If the world's zoos could actually save just 800 species, and their habitats, many current zoo critics would be less aggressive about these institutions.'
Stefan A. Omrod, former Curator of Mammals at Jersey Wildlife Preservation Trust, 1995

While zoo supporters claim that we can't possibly save thousands of endangered species from extinction without the help of zoos, their critics claim that even if every zoo in the world decided to cooperate in breeding programmes, it would be a miracle if they could save as many as 800 species. Besides, what does a rhino born and raised in a cold European city know about survival in its native countryside? Far better, zoo critics claim, to breed rhinos in protected parks in their own countries than in a foreign climate in some far-off zoo full of curious people and unnatural stresses. Is there a case to be made for captive breeding in zoos?

First you breed them...

►There's no doubt that zoos are becoming skilful in breeding animals in captivity. Sometimes their breeding programmes are so successful that zoos find themselves with a surplus of animals and are then faced with the dilemma of what to do with them. In a perfect world, careful management and constant networking with other zoos should prevent this from happening. But, as you discovered earlier, even zoos with a genuine commitment to conservation are going to breed animals that aren't endangered, not only because it's the best way to enrich the lives of adult animals in captivity, but also because these animals and their young are guaranteed crowd pullers.

What do you think?
How long do you suppose zoos would continue to breed animals simply for their box office appeal if we stopped rushing off to the zoo every time a new batch of cute babies was put on display? You have to fix in your own mind what you want zoos to be. Entertainment or conservation centres? Or a bit of both? First, though, you have to decide whether you want them at all.

The question here isn't whether zoos can breed endangered animals successfully. The best ones have the research facilities and the expertise to breed endangered animals. The question is, what's the point of breeding endangered species in zoos if wilderness areas are disappearing so fast that soon there'll be nowhere left for them to be released? A minority of zoos, the world's most reputable ones, are taking this problem very seriously. Is it too cynical a question to ask, though, whether many zoos care more about their own continued existence than about saving the world's wildlife habitats? If they can persuade people that zoos are necessary as breeding centres for the survival of endangered species, they've assured their existence well into the future. And if it turns out that there's nowhere for them to release these endangered species after they've bred them, they've still assured their existence because the only place people will be able to see these animals is in zoos.

Did you know?
In the wild, the vast majority of young animals die before reaching maturity, and generally not quickly. When animals breed in zoos, however, the standard of care and lack of predators ensure that many young survive. This means that all zoos that breed their animals inevitably end up with too many. So they either sell off the surplus to other zoos – and not always to reputable ones – to circuses or to exotic animal traders. The other option is to kill them off as humanely as possible.

Every responsible zoo director would tell you that the best way to save animals from extinction is to prevent the forests, grasslands and other wilderness areas where they live from being destroyed or taken over so that endangered animals can continue to breed in large enough numbers where they live (*in situ*), instead of having to be bred in captivity (*ex situ*). But, in defence of their captive breeding programmes, they also make a strong case that this isn't always an option. If conservationists had access to unlimited quantities of money, one solution would be to buy up vast tracts of wilderness and set up protected animal parks in them. But money for conservation purposes is in very short supply. As well, wars, expanding towns and cities, dams, land cultivation and other human activities often defeat well-intentioned plans to conserve the wilderness.

Yes, zoo critics agree, money for conservation is in short supply. So why are zoos spending money setting up captive breeding and release programmes in major cities around the world instead of investing it in wilderness conservation? Is it to justify the need for their own existence? Surely, if zoos truly had the wellbeing and survival of endangered species at heart, as many claim, they'd invest their money where it does the most good – in wilderness conservation – and use their knowledge and expertise to breed endangered species in the wild where they stand the best chance of survival?

The response from zoos is that this type of investment in endangered spaces might make sense for the conservation of small animals that need only small spaces to go about their lives. But they claim that for larger animals, for example, some rhinos, tigers, primates and a few large birds and reptiles, zoos represent the best chance of survival. Why? There are many reasons, but take tigers as one example. Several hundred tigers are required to make up a population large enough to survive in the long term, and each one of those tigers needs a territory of up to 100 sq. km. If you're going to set up a reserve for this many tigers, therefore, you'll need a chunk of land the size of Yorkshire. How many governments can you think of that are willing to set aside this much land for an animal, especially when they're under such pressure to provide land for rapidly growing human populations? Zoos maintain that the best hope for tigers is to assign them as much protected land as possible and keep their numbers up by breeding replacement tigers in zoos. Zoo critics respond that no tiger has ever been returned successfully to the wild.

> 'We are totally against captive breeding. It gives a totally false sense of security, when the truth is that this is the eleventh hour and if we don't put all our resources into saving tigers in the wild, we may lose them completely.'
> Peter Lawton, Global Tiger Control, India

. . . Then you let them go

▶Breeding an endangered species successfully in captivity is only one part of the equation. Assuming that enough of its natural habitat remains, the day will come when the zoo-bred population of the species is stable enough for some of the animals to be released into the wild. Zoo critics question whether reintroducing zoo-bred animals into the wild works well enough to justify the existence of zoo breeding programmes. They're also concerned about the possibility of zoo-bred animals carrying new strains of viruses or bacteria into populations of wild animals that have no built-in resistance to them – as almost happened in a release programme with golden lion tamarins but which, fortunately, was prevented by the zoo's screening process.

How successful have release programmes been? Not very. A study carried out in 1994 concluded that of the 145 release programmes examined, only 16 were successful. One important reason for this low success rate is that reintroduction programmes haven't been around for long and scientists are still working to perfect them. Another is that animals that have been bred and raised in the safety of the zoo don't necessarily lose their wild instincts, but they lack many of the survival skills they would have had to develop in the wild. Big cats, for instance, are born with an instinct to hunt, but they have to practise their hunting skills. Deer, meanwhile, know instinctively to stay alert to danger, but they have to learn many things about all the threats to their safety, as well as work out which plants are safe to eat. Zoo critics claim that zoo-bred animals are good for nothing besides living in zoos. But the fact that some release programmes have succeeded suggests that this isn't altogether true.

In the case of the golden lion tamarin, whose story

follows, the complicated campaign that led to its successful release included five steps:

1 Careful management of all the golden lion tamarins in zoos to produce as healthy a population as possible.
2 Research into their habits and needs to help the zoos produce conditions that would encourage the animals to breed.
3 Research into wild populations of golden lion tamarins to help the zoos train their captive animals in the ways of survival.
4 The protection, management and preservation of their jungle home.
5 Education of native people so that they knew what was being done, as well as why and what they could do to help.

Every one of these steps was vital for the success of the programme. Simply protecting the golden lion tamarin's jungle home wouldn't have been enough to save the existing populations of wild tamarins. Their small numbers and constant inbreeding had already doomed them to extinction. In the case of the golden lion tamarin (and several other animals), therefore, the role played by zoos was critical to their survival. 'A golden success story' tells how the campaign was carried out.

> **Believe it or not!**
> *A diet of pink shrimps is what makes flamingoes turn pink. Zoo flamingoes have to be fed a special additive in their food to stop them from fading.*

❑ Some wild problems

We know that animals look for three things in their natural habitat: plenty of food, a safe place to breed and a safe place to sleep and rest. In addition, big animals need plenty of space. The problem with setting up a national park in a wilderness area is that we still don't know whether the artificial boundary we set for it encircles a big enough space, let alone contains all the right kinds of feeding opportunities and safe hiding-places, to meet all the requirements of the animals we put into it. Researchers need time to be able to study wild ecosystems and learn how they operate before we start letting animals loose into ecosystems of our own choosing. Breeding and caring for animals in zoos so that they continue to survive while we gain the knowledge needed, is one way to buy researchers the time they need.

A golden success story

➤In the late 1960s as few as 600 golden lion tamarins clung to existence in isolated patches of coastal rain forest. A further 100 lived in zoos around the world. Only two per cent of the tamarin's rain forest home remained. The outlook was bleak, particularly as golden lion tamarins didn't breed successfully in captivity. (They like their privacy, and they like to choose their own lifetime mates, thank you very much.) Then, in response to a plea for help from a Brazilian scientist, a consortium of zoos, universities and conservation groups worked together to save the tamarins.

The first step was to collect all captive golden lion

tamarins into a few North American and European zoos where they could be bred under controlled conditions. The National Zoo in Washington took charge of the international studbook – a record of every captive golden lion tamarin and their bloodlines. After numerous problems had been resolved by finding out what the animals wanted and needed, the tamarins finally began to breed. By 1980, the zoo population of golden lion tamarins had doubled. If it had been allowed to grow unchecked, by 1990 there would have been 3,500 golden lion tamarins in captivity!

Next came the preparation for the really tricky part – releasing a band of 14 tamarins into the rain forest. Fortunately, Brazilian scientists had successfully negotiated a small preserve of forest to be set aside for the tamarins. In 1983 two researchers from Washington's National Zoo moved into the preserve to study the behaviour of wild golden lion tamarins and teach what they knew to Brazilian biology students who could continue their work. At the same time, local people were informed about the plight of the tamarins and asked for their support. Meanwhile, up in Washington, DC, the 14 tamarins destined for release were going through survival school. They had to learn how to leap on and off swaying branches without crashing to the ground. They were forced to search for the right kinds of food, and even had to learn how to unzip a banana.

In 1984 the small band of golden lion tamarins was taken for final jungle training to a primate centre set up by the World Wildlife Fund (US) near Rio de Janeiro. Even after all this training, half of the released tamarins were killed by predators. (This might seem shocking, but you must remember that wild species frequently suffer large losses like this.) By the middle of the following year, however, the seven survivors had produced offspring. More releases followed from the other zoos in the consortium. There are now several generations of wild-born tamarins living in the preserve that owe their existence to zoo-bred relatives. And in some cases, released animals have mated with wild tamarins, creating an even stronger gene pool.

❑ On the job with Robo-Badger

Black-footed ferrets are endangered. If you had the job of releasing them into the wild, how would you train them so that they recognize danger, and react quickly before it reaches out and bites them? The researchers trying to solve this problem decided to experiment with non-threatened, captive-bred Siberian ferrets, which are very similar to their endangered black-footed relatives. They converted an old warehouse into a replica of the ferret's natural habitat and built a remote-controlled, stuffed badger that ran on wheels. Robo-Badger's job was to stalk the ferrets among the shrubs. If a young ferret didn't run for its den the instant it saw Robo-Badger, researchers zapped it with rubber bands to speed it on its way. The results from this and other experiments are helping researchers to street-proof young black-footed ferrets before they're released.

Black rhino numbers have dropped by 96 per cent since 1970 and only 200 Siberian tigers remain.
Information from a Body Shop/Environmental Investigation Agency advertisement

What do you think?

The golden lion tamarin, like the Arabian oryx, is one of the rare success stories from zoo captive breeding programmes. Most released animals die quite soon after release because they lack the necessary survival skills. Should zoos continue to spend their money on complex breeding and release programmes or should they join forces with conservation groups to make sure that wild habitats are preserved so that endangered animals can live and breed naturally in familiar surroundings? Or should they do both?

THE ZOO AND YOU

*'The RSPCA is not opposed to zoos in principle.
It is opposed to any degree of confinement that
is likely to cause distress or suffering.'*
Colin Booty, RSPCA Wildlife Officer

Unlike factory farms and research laboratories, zoos are open to the public. This means they give you a wonderful opportunity to make your own firsthand observations about the way they treat animals and draw your own conclusions about the need for zoos. So take this book with you to the zoo and use the checklists and questions in this chapter to gather your own information.

Don't forget, however, that what you see as you stroll through the zoo is only part of what goes on there. Chances are you won't be allowed behind the scenes (unless you can somehow arrange for an official school visit) but you can ask for information on how animals are housed when they're not on display. For instance, an animal might have a spacious display enclosure full of toys and things to engage its interest, yet it might spend a large amount of time in a barren, cramped cage when it's not on display.

One of the first things you'll want to discover about the zoo you're visiting is whether it practises what it preaches. The promotional mantra of most modern zoos is 'Entertainment, Education, Conservation'. Can you find evidence of all three?

How many people do you think say to themselves, 'I'll pop along to the zoo today to find out how I can help to save endangered species.' Or, 'It's been a while since I checked out the research the zoo is doing on new strains of bamboo for pandas, maybe I should find out today.'

Precious few probably. Most people go to the zoo because they see it as a fun day out. Recent surveys say that this is so. These kinds of survey results probably make zoo public relations officers' hair stand on end. Zoos have spent years trying to change our perception of what they are all about. Strictly for entertainment? Wrong, wrong, wrong. Still able to entertain, but deeply involved in education and conservation? Better! But how true is this statement?

'Zoos are for people – they receive approximately 600 million visitors every year and turn over billions of dollars. They are primarily about entertainment.'
Will Travers, Director, Born Free Foundation, 1994

The big E: Entertainment

➤The entertainment value of a zoo is self-evident. Where else can you feel the thrill of standing eyeball to eyeball with a huge, male silverback gorilla, or a bear equipped with talons the size of daggers, safe in the knowledge that even if they charge, they can't reach you? Most of us can't afford to go on safari to exotic locations to see these animals in the wild. But at a zoo you can get so close to them you can smell them, watch them eat their dinner or socialize with each other. It's the next best thing to being in the wild. Or is it?

Animal welfare supporters claim that the way animals behave in a zoo is nothing like the way they behave in the wild. If you want to see how animals behave in the wild, they add, watch the excellent natural history films on TV because all you'll see in a zoo is a poor caricature of true animal behaviour.

Zoo supporters reply that you can't always believe everything you see in wildlife films. Sometimes situations are created deliberately to provide the film with plenty of action in the right places (and some of the action might even have been filmed in a zoo – check the credits carefully). No one would be willing to sit down and watch a 30-minute film about lions if all they did was sleep. But that's what lions do most of the day. In that respect, daylight hours for lions in a zoo aren't too far removed from a day spent in the wild. But because wildlife films cut out most of the boring bits about animals' lives, people are disappointed with the low levels of activity in a zoo.

Your chances of seeing normal animal behaviour in the best zoos improve all the time. These responsible zoos continue to look for ways to help their animals live as normal a life as possible. One reason is to make sure they don't lose their natural behaviours (this is especially important in endangered species that zoos hope one day to release into the wild), the other is so they don't develop quirky behaviours to cope with boredom or frustration.

It's easy to see how to change the way gorillas and other vegetarians feed to give them more satisfaction with their lives, but what about predators? Should zoos provide live prey for their predators to hunt and catch? Can you imagine the reaction of families who turn up for feeding time at the zoo only to watch in horror as a tiger stalks and kills a terrified baby goat? Making one animal suffer to make another feel better obviously isn't the right way to go. (Besides, it's illegal in the UK to feed a live vertebrate – that's an animal with a backbone – to another animal.) As Cologne Zoo has shown (see page 29), there are ways to give predators hunting practice and all the excitement that comes with the chase without using live prey.

❏ Signs of Madness?

On your next trip to the zoo, keep an eye open for the following signs that all is not well with its animals. Ask zoo staff whether any stereotypic behaviour you notice happens at a specific time, such as before feeding time, or whether it goes on throughout the day (a much more serious situation). Remember a minute or two's observation isn't going to provide you with enough evidence of stereotypic behaviour. So if you find an animal doing one of the things on the list below, settle down in the shade (far enough back so you don't threaten it), unpack your lunch, notepad and pencil and watch everything it does for as long as you can.

☐ **Pacing** (continuous pacing following the same route)
☐ **Neck-twisting** (unnatural movements of the neck)
☐ **Bar-biting** (gnawing on bars of cages)
☐ **Circling** (walking in circles, placing feet in same position each time)
☐ **Swaying** (side-to-side motion)
☐ **Head-bobbing** (constant up-and-down motion of head)
☐ **Tongue-playing** (repeated licking of bars or walls)
☐ **Coprophagy** (playing with or eating excrement). Be careful here. In some species, e.g. rabbits, this is normal behaviour.
☐ **Vomiting** (then eating it).
☐ **Over-grooming** (excessive licking,

grooming or hair plucking, often results in bald patches).

☐ **Self-mutilation (repeated leg or tail chewing, even head bashing).**

If you collect enough evidence of stereotypic behaviour in a zoo animal, write to the director to ask what's being done to help it.

What do you think?

Do you believe that people who are exposed to endangered animals in zoos will grow up being more willing to support campaigns to save them? How could you find proof to back up your belief?

Another pro-zoo argument claims that by exposing people to animals in zoos, we help them develop an emotional attachment to many wild species, especially endangered ones. Many children today, especially those in cities, grow up with unreal, romantic notions about animals. Is it any wonder? They've probably picked up most of their ideas from Disney-type films and cartoons, or from stories about cute and cuddly animals that act like humans in disguise.

Animals *are* like us in many respects. It would be odd if they weren't because we all belong to the animal kingdom and evolved in similar ways. Animals go about their lives in the wild, making decisions, calculating risks, taking pleasure in being warm, secure, well fed and healthy, suffering when they're cold, hungry and sick. But they're different from us too. They have no concept of right or wrong so there are no good or bad animals out there doing good or bad things. They don't lead the romantic, noble lives some of the children's books and films portray. What zoos can do is inject a healthy dollop of reality into children's – and adults' – understanding of animals. Zoos can shape visitors' attitudes towards animals through well presented education programmes. But do zoos do this? And how can you find out?

Big E no. 2: Education

►You can start by finding out what's going on at your local zoo. Without asking anyone to explain to you the zoo's education programme, see if you can figure it out. If the zoo has a competent education department, you shouldn't have much trouble. Here are some of the things to look for:

☐ Each enclosure should have an easy-to-read information board, giving you ways to make emotional contact with the animals. People feel differently about animals they know something about and are more likely to want to help them. You can stare for hours at a beautiful, exotic creature but you'll never feel connected to it unless the zoo tells you what makes it unique, how it lives and raises its young, what it eats or whether it's threatened with extinction.

☐ There should also be an explanation of any special 'cage furniture' (things like climbing apparatus, platforms, ropes, feeding dispensers, tyres, crates or traffic cones) that the zoo has introduced to the enclosure to improve the quality of the animals' lives.

☐ If a research study is in progress in an enclosure, information should be given about this too.

☐ Look around for posters, signs or displays that offer information on the work being done by the zoo to conserve endangered species. Check to see if the zoo is supporting conservation efforts in other countries. Is the zoo also involved in the conservation of wilderness areas?

☐ If you're wearing a watch, time how long people's attention is held by any single exhibit. If it's only a few seconds, they can't possibly have learned much about the animal. If possible, ask them why they didn't stay longer, and what suggestions they might have to make the exhibit grab their attention.

☐ Do you leave the zoo with a clear understanding of what you can do to help conserve endangered animals and their wilderness homes?

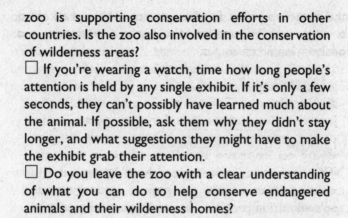

Did you know?
In 1991 the *Washington Post* surveyed zoo visitors to find out how long they looked at different animals. The Giant Panda hogged the attention for 5 minutes, the lion and rhino could only manage 1 minute, while the reptiles merited an 8-second glance each. Barely enough time to identify them let alone discover anything useful about them!

If there's little evidence of an education programme, or information is poorly presented, write to the director of the zoo and ask what he or she plans to do about it. Include any suggestions for improvement that you've gathered. If there is absolutely no attempt to educate the viewer about the animals or the need for conservation, you're probably visiting a zoo that needs considerable work from both the animal and visitor point of view. To find out how reputable your local zoo is, complete the checklist on pages 50-51. If you're able, visit several more zoos, large and small, so you can compare them with your local zoo. If you can't do that, write to them and ask them to send you information about their education and conservation programmes.

❏ Litter louts?

An incident at Edinburgh Zoo in 1994 shows just how important it is for zoos to keep the public informed about the research they're doing to improve the lives of their animals. The same day zoo researchers wrapped the chimpanzees' food in paper, management surveyed visitors to see what they thought of the zoo. The chimps spent several enjoyable hours stripping paper to get at the food. Their enclosure ended up looking like several mad games of Pass the Parcel had just taken place. And, of course, visitors were disgusted at the mess because they didn't know why it was there. If the zoo had let the public know what was going on in the enclosure, visitors would have gone away as happy as the chimps.

The big C: Conservation

➤In 1993, leading zoo people met with conservation experts to see how the two could best work together to save endangered species. They agreed that zoos are the obvious choice for global conservation centres. After all, the animals are already there, so too are the researchers and knowledgeable staff and most of the world's leading zoos already share information through the International Species Inventory System, or ISIS, which is an updated list of specimens kept and bred by zoos. They also agreed on a World Zoo Conservation Strategy, which sets out the following objectives:

1 Zoos are to work together, both in the wild and in zoos, to help save the world's endangered species and protect natural habitats and ecosystems.

2 Zoos are to share their knowledge, experience and facilities with conservationists.

3 Zoos are to help the public and governments realize the necessity for conservation and the need to rethink the use of natural resources.

These are lofty objectives for the world's 10,000 or so zoos. Unfortunately, only 500 of the world's zoos subscribe to ISIS, which means only 1 in 20 are likely to be doing anything for conservation. Is your local zoo one of them? Here's a list of questions you might like to ask its director to discover whether it's following the World Zoo Conservation Strategy.

1 What's the main purpose of the zoo? (If the answer doesn't include education, conservation and research, ask why not.)

2 Does the zoo contain many species, each represented by only a few animals? Or does it contain fewer species, each represented by many animals? (A zoo that is mostly concerned with entertainment will have the former, whereas a zoo that is serious about captive breeding will either have the latter or will be moving towards the latter.)

3 What percentage of threatened or endangered species does the zoo contain? (A zoo can't claim to be strongly involved in conservation if most of its population is under no threat of extinction. However, it takes time to humanely replace common with endangered species, so

ask about the zoo's conservation strategy.)

4 How many animals from threatened or endangered species have been born at the zoo during the past two years? (Record both number and species. Note, however, that if the zoo is part of an international breeding programme, this number can vary because of the recommendations of the programme.)

5 How many of the zoo-bred animals have been returned to the wild during the past two years? (Record both number and species. Note, however, that a zero answer does not necessarily mean the zoo isn't involved in conservation. Ask about the zoo's conservation strategy.)

6 What criteria do you use for success in release programmes?

7 Does the zoo support conservation of wild habitats? If yes, how?

8 What proportion of the zoo's income does it spend on conservation of wilderness? (Note: Find out whether the zoo receives government funding. Most UK zoos do not.)

9 How does the zoo educate the public about the animals in its care and the need for conservation?

10 What proportion of the zoo's income does it spend on research that will benefit conservation?

How to recognize the best

➤Is your local zoo up there with the best? Take this rating sheet along with you and fill it out based on what you can actually see when you visit it.

1 Physical health

a The animals look healthy and well fed with sleek coats and no sign of infection. ☐

b The animals look undernourished with poor condition coats and/or infections. ☐

2 Mental health

a The animals look alert and lively with little evidence of stereotypic behaviour. ☐

b The animals look bored or depressed and many act abnormally. (Refer to the *Signs of madness?* questionnaire you filled out on page 42.) ☐

3 Living quarters

a The animals' living spaces are large enough and contain features and equipment that allow them to exercise and play. ☐

b The animals have cramped enclosures with little or nothing in them to encourage natural behaviours. ☐

4 Social life

a The animals are grouped together as they would be in the wild. (If an animal is alone in its enclosure, find out if this is how it would normally live.) ☐

b The animals are housed with complete disregard to how they live in the wild. ☐

5 Privacy

a The enclosures are designed so that animals can have privacy when they need it. ☐

b The animals are constantly on view. ☐

6 Opportunities for natural behaviours

a The zoo gives its animals opportunities to work for their food as they would in the wild and behave in as many natural ways as possible. ☐

b The animals are fed once or twice a day with no attention paid to how they feed in the wild and have little or no opportunity to explore natural behaviours. ☐

7 Endangered species

a The zoo has a high proportion of rare or endangered species in its collection. ☐

b The zoo has few rare or endangered species in its collection. ☐

8 Serious about captive breeding

a The zoo has reduced the number of species on display but increased the number of individuals from each species. (This is often a sign of a zoo that is serious about its long-term breeding programmes.) ☐

b The zoo has a large number of species on display, each represented by a few individuals. ☐

9 Conservation

a The zoo concentrates most of its breeding efforts on endangered species. ☐

b The zoo breeds mostly non-threatened species. ☐

10 Education and research

a The zoo has an education department, which can tell you about its research and conservation programmes and which provides good information at enclosures and an inexpensive, informative guidebook. ☐

b The zoo provides little or no information about research or conservation programmes. ☐

How to rate your local zoo

For every **a)** answer score 1 point. For every **b)** answer score 0.

10 points . . . . Thumbs up! The best.
7-9 points . . . . With work can be a good zoo.
6-8 points . . . . Plenty of room for improvement.
5 points or less. . . . . . . Thumbs down!

(If the zoo scored zero on the first five questions, a call to your local authority is in order.)

> '...*captive breeding has a critical part to play in conservation for at least the next five centuries and probably more. Although today's zoos are not the ultimate centres for captive breeding, in the immediate future their role is vital.'*
> Colin Tudge, zoologist and science writer, 1995

What's your opinion now?

➤It's time to revisit the statements you considered on page 13 and find out if your reactions to them are the same now as they were before you read this section. Or, if you were unsure before, are you any closer now to having a definite opinion?

As you've no doubt noticed, the zoo issue isn't conveniently black or white. It's a horribly mixed-up shade of grey with heavy emotional overtones. So you can't just say shut them all down without worrying about what will happen to global conservation efforts if we do. Is the answer some kind of compromise? Support only the good zoos in their efforts to evolve into conservation centres while insisting that they do everything in their power to prevent their animals from suffering? Do you think zoos can put their animals' needs first and act like modern-day arks to safeguard threatened species until we can all work together to restore their wilderness homes?

One way of deciding whether zoos are needed is to ask yourself: if zoos didn't already exist, would they be one of the solutions we might come up with to save endangered species from extinction? And if so, what form should that zoo of the future take? Here are a few ideas to get you thinking.

A peek in the crystal ball

➤One new idea is to look upon a zoo as a bridge into the future. It could work like this. Zoos would cooperate worldwide to ensure the best possible success of their captive breeding programmes for endangered species. They'd keep careful records of gene pools in their studbooks so that species lines are kept pure, and continue research into the best veterinary care so that the animals remain healthy and fertile. They'd also continue to research ways to keep their animals happy. This means, of course, that the zoo would have to change its relationship with the public as it concentrates all its efforts on endangered species. Animals might take turns spending short periods of time on display so that people could continue to have emotional contact with the animals they're helping to conserve for the future. Meanwhile, the rest of the animals would be reared out of sight, and away from the stresses of human crowds, in as natural a setting as possible.

Throughout the 21st century, every effort would be made to conserve existing wilderness areas and, as the human population growth levels off and then goes into decline (at least, that's the plan), to reclaim lost habitats so that in the 22nd century – or whenever possible – zoo-bred species could be reintroduced into their natural habitats. This plan sees zoos as safe havens for between 800 and 2,000 species of animals, and perhaps also for many of the plants that share their endangered habitats. The zoo would become a Stationary Ark (a term coined by the late zoologist Gerald Durrell), carrying its precious cargo of species through time until land once more became available.

That sounds wonderful, say zoo critics, but this plan only takes care of 2,000 species at the most. There might be as many as 30 million species on Earth and it's possible that half of them could be threatened, since most live in rapidly disappearing rain forests. If 15 million species face extinction, what difference would it make if zoos save 2,000? Zoo supporters point out that land vertebrates, which excludes anything that doesn't have a backbone and doesn't live on dry land, can benefit most from captive breeding. An estimated 20,000 species of land vertebrates are threatened. And of these, approximately 2,000, including the familiar rhinos, bears, big cats, etc., need special protection through captive breeding. Seen from this perspective, what some zoos are attempting to do takes on much greater significance.

The 'time bridge' idea for zoos could carry a limited number of fully grown endangered animals forward into the future. But a 'frozen zoo' could carry test-tubes full of frozen eggs, sperm or embryos from limitless numbers of endangered species. They could be stored in liquid nitrogen at -196°C and brought to life any time in the future by defrosting the embryos and implanting them in the wombs of surrogate mothers. Quite a few animals have been born, among them cats and antelopes, which started life as a frozen embryo. And the world's first human test-tube baby, who was born in 1978, was conceived by collecting eggs from the mother, sperm from the father and mixing them together in a test-tube. The resultant embryos were then transferred to the womb of the mother and one developed naturally into a healthy baby. It wasn't quite as simple as it sounds, but that's the general idea.

Similar techniques are used in cattle, although instead of fertilizing eggs in test-tubes it's usual to flush embryos out of the wombs of their natural mothers, then transfer them into those of foster mothers. At some time in the future, it might even be possible to recreate animals from small samples of their tissue stored in a 'DNA zoo'. It brings to mind the kind of far-out science found in *Jurassic Park*, but such a tissue bank has already been started by London's Institute of Zoology.

Frozen zoos. DNA zoos. If we can develop the technology fast enough they offer less costly, less space-consuming ways of conserving today's endangered species until future generations of humans can repopulate the world's wild spaces with wild animals. But they're not exactly audience friendly, are they? You can't just pop along to either of these kinds of zoos to watch the chimps playing with their food. Maybe what's needed is a Cyber Zoo that you can tour by donning a virtual reality headset. Don't laugh, this isn't as far-fetched as it sounds. In fact, visitors to Zoo Atlanta can already have a taste of the Cyber Zoo of the future. When they put on a virtual reality headset they're transformed into an adolescent member of a group of gorillas living in a replica of the zoo's gorilla enclosure. It doesn't take long to find out what annoys the adult male in your group! And you know you've arrived as a gorilla when the adult female offers to groom you.

So there you are, left with a decision to make. Traditional zoos. Conservation zoos. Frozen zoos. DNA zoos. Or no zoos. It's up to you.

QUIZ

Would you know an endangered animal if you met one?

Do you know how many of these popular zoo animals are in trouble? Give each one a rating based on the explanation below.

***** = endangered and likely to become extinct.

**** = endangered and likely to become extinct but small populations of them survive in zoos or reserves.

*** = some but not all subspecies or species are endangered or their numbers have declined over most of their range.

** = naturally rare and therefore vulnerable or they're OK but their habitat is threatened.

* = there's some concern for them but they're not immediately threatened.

Animal species	*****	****	***	**	*
Panda					
Lion					
Tiger					
Rhinoceros					
Leopard					
Polar Bear					
Gorilla					
Orangutan					
Chimpanzee					
Elephant					
Giraffe					
Zebra					

(Answers page 223)

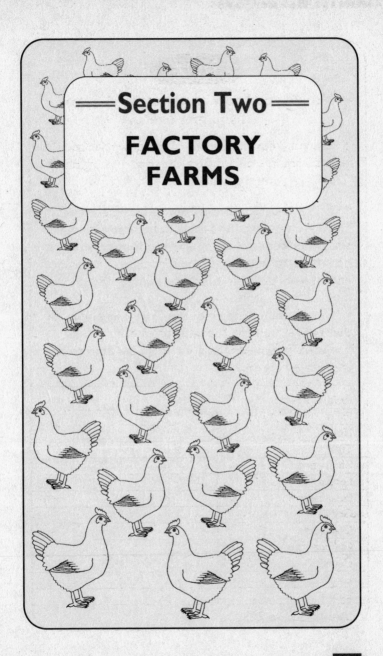

Section Two

FACTORY FARMS

'The time will come when men such as I will look upon the murder of animals as they now look upon the murder of men.'
Leonardo da Vinci

On a bleak January day in 1998, the Tamworth Two made their break for freedom. They had nothing to lose in the attempt and their timing was perfect. They had already found a weak spot in the perimeter fence before the alarm was raised and it took only seconds to wriggle under the fence to freedom. But they quickly had to put some distance between themselves and the men who would soon turn out in force to hunt them down, which meant only one thing. They had to cross the River Avon. Finding a bridge was out of the question – the pair plunged headlong into the hostile, swollen waters and struck out desperately for the far shore. Numb with cold but driven by fear, they battled on until finally they felt solid ground under their feet. Quickly they hauled themselves out of the river and ran for cover.

If you followed the news that month, you'd know that the Tamworth Two were later apprehended. And you'd also know that they weren't escaped terrorists or hardened criminals, but two five-month-old Tamworth pigs who took one look at a slaughterhouse in Malmesbury and decided it wasn't for them. The media worked overtime on one pun-filled story after another. The Tamworth Two were quickly dubbed Butch Cassidy and the Sundance Pig, after the two American bank-robbing folk heroes who made an equally desperate run for their lives. It didn't take long before the story was also carried on American and French TV. Offers of sanctuary for the two pigs flooded in, and millions of people waited anxiously to learn their fate.

Butch was the first to be captured on Tetbury Hill by an

exhausted, muddied group of reporters, who whisked her off to safety. Slowly the net closed on Sundance, who took refuge in a thicket. His human captors were no match for the thorns so they sent in a dog to flush him out. Even so, it took eight strong men and the local vet to subdue him.

That night a policeman stood guard outside the vet's surgery where Sundance was recovering from his ordeal, and the next day he was reunited with Butch at a nearby animal sanctuary. (A newspaper bought the pigs for a reputed £15,000 and promised to let them live out the rest of their days in comfort and safety. In the spring, the famous twosome moved into their permanent home at The Wildside Trust's Badzel Park in Kent, where they have all possible pig mod cons, including a large, thatched pig sty, a mud wallow and plenty of earth to root in, as well as some interesting porcine neighbours.) People around the world let out a collective sigh of relief.

Don't you think there's something slightly skewy going on here? If we can feel so compassionate towards two pigs that make a break for freedom, why don't we feel the same way towards the millions of pigs that don't? Apparently a third pig had attempted to escape and didn't make it. According to the slaughterhouse, it was 'processed in the usual way'. This pig had no name and therefore no identity and no call on our sympathy. It hadn't shown how desperate it was to survive, so we were content to let it be processed like a tin of peas. (The Tamworth Two are very inquisitive, active pigs. They weren't raised in a factory farm – the modern system of intensive farming where thousands of animals are reared in artificial, often inhumane, conditions indoors. Could this have been what gave them their streak of independence?)

A few years ago, we were shocked into awareness of what happens to animals inside factory farms when graphic

This book is due for return on or before the last date shown below.

scenes from an egg factory were broadcast on TV. But chickens aren't the only animals that are raised in factory farms. Turkeys, pigs, dairy and beef cattle and veal calves are all treated like cogs in a machine rather than aware beings that care about what happens to them. Is this any way to treat animals?

What's your opinion?
Don't worry if you can't make up your mind, you'll have a chance later to make a decision.

It's OK to kill animals for food, providing we cause them as little suffering as possible.
I agree ☐   I disagree ☐   I'm not sure   ☐

We are doing everything possible to make sure animals don't suffer in factory farms.
I agree ☐   I disagree ☐   I'm not sure   ☐

Without factory farms, meat and dairy produce would be too expensive.
I agree ☐   I disagree ☐   I'm not sure   ☐

The best way to help farm animals is to become a vegetarian.
I agree ☐   I disagree ☐   I'm not sure   ☐

The choices we all make in food shops have an impact on the welfare of farm animals.
I agree ☐   I disagree ☐   I'm not sure   ☐

What supporters of factory farming say:
- Factory farming is the only economic way we can keep millions of animals safe, warm, well fed and watered.
- Factory farm animals are healthier because they can be checked and treated quickly.
- Factory farming makes cheap meat and dairy products available to everyone.
- Animals born and raised in factory farms don't miss what they've never had.

What critics of factory farming say:
- Factory farms treat animals like production machines.
- Animals suffer physically and emotionally in factory farms.
- Factory farms damage the environment.
- We have no right to make animals suffer so that we can have cheap food.

Why did we turn farms into food factories?

➤In the years immediately following World War II, Britain was short of both food and manpower. Food and other essential goods had to be rationed so that everyone had a fair share. Even so, people began to suffer the effects of poor nutrition. We needed a way to cheaply produce large quantities of food using far less labour than was possible on traditional farms. In other words, farms had to become more like factories where food could be mass-produced. In 1953 two things happened that made this possible: antibiotics became generally available and feed for livestock was no longer rationed.

The discovery of antibiotics meant that for the first time farmers could house large numbers of animals together indoors without fear of them all being wiped out by a deadly disease. And with the promise of plenty of food for their animals, farmers could increase the size of their flocks and herds. No wonder the government encouraged farmers to give up their traditional, labour-intensive (but greener and more humane) methods for the new, super-efficient farming systems of the future.

It all seemed so positive then. At last, there was a chicken for every pot and people could stop eating margarine made from whale blubber and swap powdered eggs and milk for the real things. As nutrition improved, so too did people's health. It wasn't until many years later that we began to read in the papers about traces of hormones or antibiotics in our food, or about the impact that factory farming was having on the environment. Only then did we begin to question the wisdom of moving so far away from traditional farming methods. Later still, we began to worry about the kind of impact factory farming had on animals.

PIGS 'N' HENS

> *'Most people find the sight of pigs or chickens, reared under ... conditions more appropriate to vegetables than to animals, deeply disturbing, and this feeling ought surely to be respected.'*
> Roger Scruton, writer and philosopher, 1966

Several years ago, when we began to realize that what we put in our mouths could affect how soon we had our first heart attack, it became fashionable to eat low-cholesterol white meat rather than beef, which had more fat in it then than it does today. As demand for meat from pigs and chicken went up, their fate was sealed. Any chance of them being thought of as individuals was lost as they often literally fought for survival in dark, overcrowded sheds.

Bacon machines

➤If you could go back about 900 years and stroll through the dense forests that still covered much of Britain, you'd eventually come across wild pigs – thousands of them. (People began domesticating pigs as long ago as the Stone Age, but they continued to live wild in the woods until the middle of the 18th century.) They rooted around in woodlands, digging up roots, beechmast, acorns and vegetation, helping to keep the soil fertile by turning it over and mixing in rotting leaves. This instinct of pigs to root and find food that other animals miss helped them to survive for 40 million years without any assistance from us. In the wild, pigs live in small groups of females and youngsters called sounders, while older male pigs, called boars, usually live alone. Female pigs, called sows, build cosy nests for their young and help each other when needed. If a mother sow calls a warning, for instance, her piglets freeze and other females rush in to protect them.

> *Believe it or not!*
> *One captive bush pig found a hairline crack in the floor of his concrete enclosure. It took him only a few hours of hard rooting to break up the concrete!*

Pigs are intelligent animals. 'It may sound strange, but I've watched pigs stand back and think about a problem,' said a researcher into pig behaviour at Plymouth University. And another professor at Pennsylvania State University has adapted computer games for pigs. He's trying to figure out whether pigs kept locked up in small spaces are capable of wanting to be somewhere else. People who have worked with pigs say they can be trained just like dogs. (Could there be some truth to the film *Babe*?) No matter how intelligent pigs might be, however, some farming systems have been treating them like mindless bacon-producing machines since 1966, the year swine fever was conquered in Britain and pigs could be intensively raised indoors.

❑ The Five Freedoms
Several years ago the UK Farm Animal Welfare Council (FAWC) stated that any farm animal should have:

1 freedom from hunger and thirst
2 freedom from discomfort
3 freedom from pain, injury or disease
4 freedom to express normal behaviour
5 freedom from fear and distress

These Five Freedoms, as they became known, identify the basic needs of animals and try to make the best of a very complex situation. You can use them to gauge how well pigs, hens and cattle fare in intensive farming situations. (You can also use them to see how well animals are doing in a zoo or a research laboratory – or even in your own home.)

A sow spends most of her life pregnant, giving birth to her first litter when she's just under a year old. In most pig units throughout Europe, pregnant sows are kept in stalls about as wide as the seat in an armchair but nowhere near as comfortable. The floor is often concrete so that it's easy to hose down and sometimes the sow is tethered to it by a chain. She can move one pace forwards or backwards, stand up or lie down. But she can't turn around. And she can't wander off to find a nice cool mud-hole to wallow in when she feels like it.

When she's ready to give birth, or farrow, the sow is moved into a farrowing crate even narrower than the sow stall. It contains little bedding, so the sow can't follow her very strong instinct to build a nest. The bars of the crate are arranged to create a space off to one side for the piglets so that they're not crushed by their mother when she struggles to lie down. (In the wild, of course, this isn't usually a problem because wild pigs don't put on as much weight as domestic pigs or have such large litters.) Soon after the piglets are weaned at about four weeks of age, the sow is mated once again and has to repeat the whole pregnancy–birth–suckling cycle every 5 months, producing 20 or more piglets each year.

> **Did you know?**
> Like their distant relatives, hippopotamuses, pigs use mud to cool down and protect their sensitive skins from sunburn.

If the piglets were allowed to wean themselves naturally, they'd continue suckling for up to three months – keeping their mother out of production far too long. So they're taken from her as early as possible and kept in heated cages until they're old enough to be fattened up for market. Most growing pigs are kept indoors in pens so that they don't have to waste food and energy staying warm. By crowding in as many animals as possible and keeping the lights low, farmers prevent pigs from moving around too much, so they quickly put on weight. (Did you know that 48 piglets were needed to make *Babe* because they all grew too fast?)

The lucky ones are raised in spacious buildings with straw bedding that's replenished frequently. The unlucky ones are fattened up in 'sweat boxes' with no bedding and a concrete floor. If growing pigs can't play or root around in straw or earth, they quickly become bored and stressed. And stressed pigs get into fights. Some farmers remove the sharp points of their pigs' teeth so they don't seriously injure each other. Many farmers cut off their tails because they're easy targets for bites.

> *When an American pig producer was asked what he thought about cutting off pigs' tails he replied: 'They hate it! The pigs just hate it! And I suppose we could do without tail-docking if we gave them more room, because they don't get crazy and mean when they have more space. With enough room, they're actually quite nice animals. But we can't afford it. These buildings cost a lot.'*

❏ A soft-hearted diamond

Farmers have known for a long time that when you put too many pigs together in the same space they'll fight because overcrowding is very stressful to them. New animal welfare laws (enforced in 1999) make it illegal to house sows in single pens and so they have to live together in barns or yards. Anticipating the mayhem that could result, a Gloucester company spent ten years perfecting a new breed of pig. She's known as the Cotswold Diamond and she's special because she's extremely sweet natured and gets on well with other pigs. Animal welfare researchers see this as a step forward, but caution farmers that even the sweetest pigs will eventually lose their tempers if too many of them are crammed into the same space.

What do you think?

What do you think of a solution that ignores the problem – overcrowding – but instead makes pigs adjust better to living in stressful conditions? Can we go on thinking we can fix everything with science and technology without even acknowledging that maybe pigs have an interest in what happens to them?

Is there a better life for pigs?

➤Pigs are born rooters. They can't help themselves, they have to do it. Just how much was demonstrated in an experiment in which pigs were offered a choice between food and a tray full of dirt. That's right, they chose to root in the dirt rather than eat the food. To satisfy one of their pigs' basic instincts, therefore, farmers should make sure they have plenty of opportunities to root for their food.

Some farmers keep their pigs in fields and provide small sheds or 'arks' where the pigs can shelter from bad weather or too much sun. Living outdoors like this gives pigs plenty of opportunity to root in the earth – providing the farmer doesn't equip them with nose rings, which give pigs painful snouts when they attempt to dig. The irony of being set free in a field then being prevented from digging might be lost on the pig, but the frustration certainly isn't. If a farmer allows his pigs to root, provides extra shade and mud wallows during the summer, and plenty of straw bedding and good field drainage during the winter, the ark system scores well for all Five Freedoms.

❑ Piggy preferences

Research shows that we don't always know what's best for animals. Two researchers wanted to find out how much light pigs prefer to have so they trained them to turn lights on and off by breaking an infrared beam with their snouts. The pigs made their desires perfectly clear: they wanted much more light than farmers were giving them, even some at night. In another experiment, even untrained pigs quickly learned to switch on a heater.

If a farmer can't provide outdoor arks for pigs, he or she can house them in covered, well-strawed yards. They protect the pigs from bad weather and if the farmer provides plenty of clean straw each day, his pigs will happily root in it and eat it. In the outdoor ark system, pigs rarely fight because they can get away from each other. In covered yards, fights usually break out over food. A cheap, natural solution would be to scatter food pellets all over the straw yard. Pigs that have to root around to find their own food are usually much too busy to think about fighting. Many farmers like this system, but worry that it doesn't allow them to give extra food to pigs that might need it.

Egg machines

►Imagine you're making a dangerous trek through a tropical jungle in the dead of night. As you raise your machete to hack a path through the dense undergrowth, be careful that you don't smash into one of the low branches overhead. You could disturb a small flock of jungle fowl, maybe a cockerel and five or six hens, that are roosting there for the night. At daybreak when all the night prowlers have crawled back into their dens, jungle fowl leave their roost and fly down to the forest floor, where they'll spend the day busily foraging for food. When it's time to lay their eggs, the hens find well hidden, hard-to-reach places and build themselves comfortable nests.

The eggs you eat for breakfast come from hens that have evolved from jungle fowl. Until the 1950s and the growth of factory farms, farmyard hens were able to act just like their distant jungle ancestors. They spent the night roosting together in small groups on perches in a hen-house where they were safe from foxes and weasels. When the cockerel greeted the sunrise, they left their roost and spent the day foraging for food around the farmyard. If they wanted to clean their feathers they found a patch of dirt and enjoyed a good dust-bath. When a hen felt the urge to find a nesting site, she went into the hen-house and settled into a straw-lined nesting box.

In most of today's factory farms, laying hens never see a farmyard let alone a nesting box, nor do they have a chance to take a dust-bath. Laying hens are kept in small, wire cages stacked as many as six high down both sides of a windowless shed. Inside, the lights stay on 17 hours a day because this length of 'day' stimulates the hens to lay more eggs – as many as 280 or more a year. (To appreciate what an achievement this is, you should know that wild jungle fowl normally lay only about 65 eggs a year.)

As many as five birds are crammed into each cage, giving each one a floor space slightly smaller than one page out of a school notebook. Spreading their wings is out of the question. And because they can't get away from each other, they often fight. One way to keep the aggression levels low is to dim the lights. So the hens spend their 'days' in perpetual twilight before being plunged into darkness for seven hours of 'night'. Of course, the sun could be shining outside when it's night-time in the shed but the hens will never know. The only time they see the sky is when they're shipped out for slaughter. And bright sunlight can so alarm them that farmers often ship them out at night.

> '**Attention to animal welfare and successful poultry farming go hand-in-hand.'**
> **National Farmers Union, 1994**

An egg battery is set up for maximum efficiency. Each cage is equipped with an automatic water dispenser. The shed is well ventilated and the temperature is maintained between 21°C and 24°C – the best temperature for egg-laying. Three sets of conveyor belts run the length of the shed. One carries food, one removes bird droppings that fall through the wire bottoms of the cages and the third takes away the eggs as they roll off the sloping floors of the cages.

How do millions of birds, whose instincts probably still tell them they should be strutting around the jungle floor with a few of their mates, survive for a whole year in such artificial conditions? A chicken's feet are designed for walking on solid ground and wrapping around branches. Forcing laying hens to stand or sit on wire mesh all their lives damages their feet. In extreme cases, birds have been found welded to the wire mesh because the flesh of their deformed feet have grown around it.

It's difficult to know whether laying hens suffer more physical than emotional pain. For more than 280 days of the year they suffer the frustration of not being able to find a quiet nesting box to lay their eggs. And they're also denied the opportunity to dust-bathe to rid their feathers of parasites. (Can you imagine having to go for a year without a bath?) Dust-bathing is such a strong instinct that battery hens pretend they're doing it on the bare wire floors of their cages. Frustrated, they often end up pecking at each other until they bleed. Once blood is drawn, the pecking can escalate, causing severe injury or death. Caged hens have even resorted to cannibalism. By the time a hen comes to the end of her egg-laying career, which is usually after a year, she is probably in constant pain from her injured feet. And because she's had absolutely no exercise, chances are she's also suffering from liver disease and brittle bones that break easily.

❏ Ban the batteries

In July 1997 the government announced plans to phase out battery systems and develop more humane systems of egg production. It could take ten or more years to achieve this goal because the Ministry of Agriculture, Food and Fisheries wants to campaign for a Europe-wide ban. It has been estimated that an area the size of Wiltshire would be needed to house the free range hens that might replace battery hens, and the move to free range could increase the price of eggs by 14 per cent. (An extra 20p or so on 12 eggs might not seem like much, but to shoppers whose food budget is already stretched to the limit, such a large price increase on a staple food item is not good news.) Free range and perchery egg production systems provide more opportunities for freedom for laying hens, but they're not perfect either. More research is needed to find a combination of systems, that assures the welfare of hens but still allows farmers to make a fair profit so they don't have to hand on large price increases to the consumer.

> *The main reason free range eggs cost slightly more than battery eggs is that many consumers are demanding what few farmers are supplying. As supply and demand equal out, the cost will drop.*

Drumsticks or nuggets?

►Next time you're in a supermarket, pick up a pack of chicken parts and try to imagine the bird they came from. Difficult isn't it? Even whole chickens are cut, trussed up and packaged so that they bear no resemblance to something that once would have been at home on the jungle floor. And fast food outlets go even further to disguise the fact that you're eating flesh from a bird that once had feathers and wings, even if it wasn't allowed to flap them. What part of a chicken do nuggets come from? No wonder we think of chickens as anonymous cogs in a production wheel, if we think of them at all. Now take a guess at how many chickens are reared and killed in the UK each year. 70 million? 370 million? Try 760 million – at least that's how many were produced in 1996, the last year for which figures were published before this book went to press. And most of them were raised in huge, windowless sheds known as broiler houses.

Did you know?
Animal welfare codes recommend that chickens and turkeys are debeaked only as a last resort to prevent injury or death in overcrowded situations. Yet almost a third of battery hens, three-quarters of breeder hens and almost all turkeys have a third of their upper beak burned off 'as a last resort'. Why don't animal welfare codes do something about overcrowding instead – the true cause of the problem?

Unlike laying hens, broiler chickens are free to roam around the shed floor, which is usually covered in straw or wood shavings. It sounds as if they have a much better life, doesn't it? However, there's a catch. Like hens, each broiler chicken is allotted 450 sq. cm of floor space. This might be room enough for a day-old-chick, but thanks to a rich diet and drugs that turn them into superchickens that grow much faster than normal, by the time 50,000 or even 100,000 fluffy yellow chicks in one broiler house are ready for slaughter less than two months later, conditions have changed dramatically. For a start, they can weigh more than four times the size of the average laying hen of the same age, which makes conditions on the broiler floor acutely claustrophobic.

> **What do you think?**
> Are we wrong to interfere with the normal growth rate of chickens (and pigs) if in doing so we make them suffer?

In 1996 more than 45 million birds died in the sheds – suffocated, choked or trampled to death in the urine-soaked litter underfoot. Maybe they were the lucky ones. The survivors have to continue putting up with the noise, the smell and the constant stress of too many bodies wanting the same space, and often go on to develop painful leg problems because they're not built to support such rapid weight growth. In extreme cases, birds can hardly move and have trouble reaching food and water. Others suffer from ammonia burns caused by standing on the filthy litter, which is cleaned out once – after the birds have been shipped off for slaughter. Still others develop breathing problems from the ammonia. And pity the poor birds who have the misfortune of being grown for the Christmas season. Because, like turkeys, who also have to be kept longer to reach a larger size, they'll probably also suffer chronic pain from having their beaks seared off to prevent them killing each other.

Did you know?
Our preference for the less-fattening white meat on our Christmas turkey has resulted in turkeys being bred to have such huge breast muscles that they can no longer mate or fly. (Wild turkeys can reach speeds of up to 80 km/h.)

Chickens deserve better too!

➤ Check out the eggs in your local supermarket. Anything that's not marked as free range, perchery/aviary or barn eggs came out of a battery (probably marketed as 'farm fresh'). In a free range system, the hens are shut up in a hen-house or shed at night to protect them from predators, but are allowed outside during the day. In many ways, the free range system is kinder than the battery system because it gives hens the opportunity to act much more naturally. They can walk about and scratch for food when they feel like it. However, the larger the free range system, the fewer the benefits it offers to hens.

Did you know?
Not all free range systems are as free as they sound. As many as 4,000 hens might live in a large shed with 'pop' holes leading outside. Very few birds, however, might want to pop outside, especially if they are fed inside. Why? There might be too few holes. They might be guarded by bully birds that stop others using them. Or the hens, still having the instinct of wild jungle fowl, might be afraid of open, barren spaces.

In the perchery/aviary or barn system, large flocks of birds are kept in houses or sheds that usually contain several tiers of perches and lined nest boxes. The hens are free to nest, perch and wander inside the shed. Litter, made up of wood shavings, straw, sand or turf, is provided so that the hens can scratch in it and use it for dust-bathing. These are definite improvements over the battery system. However, if too many birds are housed together, fights will break out over living space and food, and most hens in overcrowded conditions are debeaked. And unless the litter is kept in good condition, a build up of ammonia can cause problems for the birds.

❑ What do hens want?

Animal welfare researchers have spent a lot of time trying to discover the answer to this question. Here's what their research shows:

- Hens prefer living in small groups of four or five birds.
- They prefer foraging for their own food rather than having it provided.
- Scratching and pecking opportunities are a must.
- Having to approach a group of strange birds makes hens nervous.
- Nest boxes are vitally important to laying hens. (In one experiment, hens even squeezed through narrow spaces, which they hate to do, to reach a nest box when it was time to lay an egg.)
- Hens won't work as hard for a dust-bath as they will for a nest box, so they might consider it a pleasant extra rather than a necessity.

Farmers who satisfy these basic needs have taken a giant step towards treating their hens humanely.

Unfortunately for broiler chickens, there is currently no alternative to being raised on litter in large, windowless sheds. Conditions for all chickens — whether laying, breeding or broiler — could be improved by giving each bird considerably more floor space. The government recommendation of a space smaller than the cover of a telephone directory for each broiler chicken in the last week of its life is woefully inadequate.

> *More space, clean litter, nest boxes, perches and the opportunity to get away from others and live a more natural life — that's what alternative systems should offer. And if the chickens and eggs that come out of these kinder systems cost a little more money, we should be willing to pay it for their sake.*

What do you think?
Would most people be prepared to pay more money for bacon and eggs if it meant giving pigs and chickens more living space and a better quality of life? Would you?

SHEEP 'N' COWS

Sheep have a reputation, even if it's not deserved, of being incredibly stupid. Be that as it may, sheep are the only ones out of the big four of modern farming — pigs, chickens, cattle and sheep — that have managed to keep themselves out of factory farms. How? They are marvels at converting very poor grass into high energy protein. In fact, they help farmers profit from pastures that aren't fit enough for other crops. Their thin, flexible lips and narrow mouths even allow them to reach plants that cattle can't crop. So it simply doesn't make sense to bring them indoors into an intensive breeding system.

However, just because sheep are free to behave naturally, and so don't really belong in a book about animals behind bars, doesn't mean they lead happy, healthy lives. Many neglected sheep die from starvation, whether they're hill sheep in Britain or belong to one of the vast flocks of wool sheep in Australia. Foot-rot is a horrible but all-too-common ailment and blowfly strike is an appalling affliction in which sheep can be eaten alive by maggots. Sheep sometimes pay a high price for their freedom and they deserve as much attention from animal welfare activists as pigs, poultry and cows. And what about cows? Aren't they also free to live almost normal lives as they graze contentedly in lush pastures? Not quite.

Hamburgers 'n' milkshakes

►Somehow, when you sang '*Old MacDonald Had a Farm*' as a child and you reached the moo-moo part, you just knew Old MacDonald had a cow called Daisy. All farmers had a cow called Daisy, didn't they? Cows were given names in the days when they were brought in from the pasture each afternoon to be milked by hand. Having a name helped humans see them as individuals with likes and dislikes, just as the names Butch Cassidy and the Sundance Pig changed two anonymous Tamworth pigs into characters that people cared about. Many farmers might still name their favourite dairy cows but the way they have to farm these days makes this less and less likely.

The problem for dairy cows in factory farms isn't so much overcrowding, it's exhaustion from being pushed to their physical limit every day to produce more milk than ever before. By selecting and breeding only good milk-producing cows, farmers have created a modern dairy cow that produces ten times more milk than her calf needs. And instead of being milked by hand, she's milked twice a day by a machine. The size of the udder required to store 20 litres of milk forces the cow to alter the natural position of her back legs, resulting in painful lameness, and the enlarged udder is prone to painful inflammation known as mastitis. (If you want to know what it feels like to be a modern dairy cow, try standing around all day with a football between your thighs!) The demands on today's dairy cow are so huge that many cows, which normally could expect to live 20 years, are worn out by the time they're five. So they're slaughtered and their tough meat is used in beef pies and hamburgers.

> **Believe it or not!**
> **To equal the amount of work done by a dairy cow when she's producing her maximum amount of milk, you'd have to jog for about six hours a day, every day.**

It's true that dairy cows live in better conditions than pigs or hens during the summer months. After all, it can't be too bad grazing on lush green grass in beautiful countryside, especially when the weather's good. There's plenty of space to avoid the bullies, a field full of food to eat where and when one chooses, things going on around to look at and investigate, and opportunities to do natural cow things. But what happens when the winter comes?

Dairy cows used to be housed each winter in barns or covered yards, both supplied with plenty of straw. As specialized factory farms took over from traditional farms, however, straw became either hard to find or too expensive to bring in from elsewhere. The solution was to house cattle in buildings with either concrete or slatted floors, both of which are easier to keep clean than a straw-covered floor that has to be regularly mucked out.

Farm-hands might not have enjoyed mucking out traditional straw bedding, but dairy cows certainly approved of it. Cows kept in straw yards suffer far less from lameness and infections than those kept on slatted floors. Some dairy cows, especially in American herds, are kept indoors all year round in a farming system known as 'zero grazing'. They eat silage – grass that is stored in a silo until bacterial action begins to break it down – with added high protein foods. One drawback to silage is that it produces semi-liquid droppings that can become a serious pollutant.

Did you know?
Research shows that when cattle are offered a choice between having bedding materials in their stalls or having the temperature raised, they'll choose a comfy bed even when the temperature dips as low as -20°C.

Daisy's babies

►The only way a dairy cow can produce milk is to first produce a calf. More than half a million calves are born in the UK every year so that we can put milk on our cereal. Their purpose is to stimulate milk production in their mothers and their job is finished when they're one day old. They are then taken away from their mothers. Some of the female calves are bucket fed milk or 'milk replacer' plus easily digestible dry feed so that they can be weaned off their milk diet as early as four weeks of age. These calves will become future milk producers. (It's ironic, isn't it, that a dairy cow is expected to produce 20 litres of milk for our consumption every day, yet was allowed to suckle her mother, and drink the milk that by rights should have been hers, for only the first day of her life?)

Male calves are no use at all to the dairy herd and so they're quickly sold off at auction as veal calves. Some are raised in the UK, the rest are exported to other countries in Europe. This means that calves only a few days old are put through the frightening experience of being transported to auction before possibly being shipped abroad, where they will spend their short lives imprisoned in individual wooden crates with bare, slatted floors. During this time, they have no room to move around or exercise, they can't play with other calves, they have very little light, no iron in their liquid diet and no roughage. They aren't even given any straw to lie on in case they eat it as roughage. This inhumane treatment of calves produces white, tender meat that's highly sought after by restaurants when they are slaughtered at six months of age.

❏ Do we have to be cruel to be kind?

How can farmers be so cruel as to take a calf away from its mother when it's only one day old? Farmers have a difficult job to do and if they became sentimental about their animals they'd soon go out of business. Many have learned the hard way that it's less cruel to take a calf away from its mother just after it's born than wait until the pair have had an opportunity to form a strong emotional bond.

Some dairy farmers, however, prefer to sell their calves when they're about eight weeks old. They might house the calves separately from their mothers but allow them to suckle twice a day for up to three weeks. This mimics what happens in wild cattle, when mothers protect their calves during the day by leaving them hidden in the grass away from the herd, only seeing them at feeding times. In the dairy herd, both mothers and calves are content with this arrangement so long as it continues. But the longer it lasts, the more painful is the separation.

Beef stew

➤If those aren't dairy cows and their calves you see grazing in the fields, what are they? They're 'suckler' beef cows and they produce half of all the beef in the UK. (The other half comes from calves born to dairy cows and raised artificially.) The mothers are allowed to suckle their calves because this is the most efficient way of raising a big, meaty calf. And that's the main goal of each suckler cow: to hand over the largest possible calf for slaughter each year before she goes to the slaughterhouse herself at the end of her productive life.

When it comes to calf production, little is left to chance. Suckler cows don't mate with bulls. They receive implants of two or more embryos that are taken from special donor cows. While the dairy bull is chosen because he produces daughters that give large quantities of milk, the beef bull is chosen because he's big and meaty and will probably sire large calves. The farmer ensures that the calf lives up to its beefy potential by allowing it to suckle its mother's milk for as long as eight months until it's naturally weaned. The calf's short life might be relatively sweet but its mother has a longer, tougher life. Suckler cows frequently suffer birthing problems because their calves are too large.

What do you think?

Some suckler cows, such as the Belgian Blue, which are specially bred for their oversized muscles, have to give birth by Caesarian section year after year. This carries a high risk of chronic abdominal pain. To reduce the risk of problems at calving, farmers sometimes reduce the birthing weight of calves by cutting the food rations of their mothers to the point where they are thin and hungry at calving time. How much can we and farmers and agricultural researchers ethically ask a cow to endure just for enjoyment and profit?

❏ Mad scientist disease

In the past, straw soaked in urine and droppings was raked out of the cow barn and thrown on to the manure heap. Heat build-up in the manure heap eventually killed off harmful organisms so that the well-rotted manure could be dug back into the fields as fertilizer. Today, manure from hens is just as likely to find its way into cattle food. Researchers seemed surprised when cows turned up their noses at food containing poultry manure. It's a pity cows didn't refuse to eat sheep offal when it was put in their food. Then we would never have heard of mad cow disease.

How can we be kinder to cows?

➤The biggest problems dairy cows have to face – apart from the fact that none of them are raised naturally by their mothers – have to do with the amount of milk they're pressed to produce and the impact this has on their health. In future, a dairy cow might be able to walk into an automatic milking station four to six times a day and have a robotic arm place milking cups on her teats. Being able to be milked on demand would be a boon to cows. It would reduce the size of their udders and so help prevent both lameness and painful udder infections. It would be a boon to farmers, too, because the more a cow is milked, the more she produces. Increased milk production, however, would prove even more exhausting for dairy cows if they weren't given improved diets and plenty of opportunity for rest to make up for the extra workload on their bodies.

After a public outcry, Britain outlawed veal crates on 1 January 1990, but they are still used in the rest of Europe and the United States. British farmers are allowed to keep single calves in pens or stalls providing they are roomy enough. And if the calf is more than 14 days old, in addition to bucket-fed milk substitute, the calf must also have access to food containing roughage. After eight weeks, the calves must be housed in groups. Unfortunately, the pens often have floors of concrete slats. Understandably, it's not long before the calves are filthy and injured from slipping on the dung-slimed slats.

A kinder way to rear veal calves is to pen them in groups of 20 on deep straw in covered yards. The straw provides a comfy bed and roughage when they eat it. They can play with each other and exercise or rest when they feel like it. They can also feed when they're hungry at an automatic milk-feeder, which pumps warm milk to artificial teats inside the pen. Giving veal calves an opportunity to satisfy their instinctive urge to suck helps to prevent them developing abnormal behaviours, such as sucking each others' tongues.

Did you know?
Following the UK ban on the use of veal crates in 1990, the EU has now agreed to ban them by the end of 2006, except in new or renovated buildings for which the ban came into force on 1 January 1998.

Adding up the scores

➤How many of the Five Freedoms do factory farms allow animals? As you can see from the table opposite, there's a tell-tale divide between freedoms that help production and freedoms that help the animal. Keeping animals well fed and watered, as well as warm and free from disease, makes good business sense because it helps boost production. With the exception of the disease rates among cattle, factory farms score well in these categories. But they score poorly in three other categories: freedom from pain, freedom to behave normally and freedom from fear and distress. These are the freedoms that animal welfare activists are demanding on behalf of farm animals. Production doesn't suffer through the lack of them, only the animals suffer.

Freedom	Battery hens	Broilers	Pigs	Cattle	Veal calves
from hunger and thirst	✓	✓✓	✓✓	✓	✗
from cold	✓✓	✓✓	✓✓	✓✓	✓✓
from discomfort	✗	✓	✗	✗	✗
from disease	✓	✓✓	✓	✗✗	✓
from pain	✗	✗	✗	✗	✗
to act normally	✗✗	✗	✗	✗	✗✗
from fear and distress	✗	✗	✗	✗	✗✗

✓✓ Good   ✓ Adequate   ✗ Poor   ✗✗ Very poor

THE FINAL CRUELTY

'As long as there are slaughterhouses there will be battlefields.'
Leo Tolstoy

There comes a time in the lives of all farm animals when they have either outlived their usefulness – as in the case of a worked-out dairy cow or spent laying hen – or they have achieved their ideal weight for market and are ready for eating. One day, the doors of the shed will be flung open and the animals will be pushed into crates or forced up ramps into transport lorries. No doubt you've seen these animal carriers on the road, maybe even been stuck next to one in a tailback on the motorway. Sometimes the animals are crammed in so tightly they cannot move, let alone lie down to rest. If it's a hot day they'll suffer from heat and dehydration. And they'll probably be hungry.

The thinking seems to be, why feed an animal that's about to die? They might have been on the road for hours, with many more hours or even days to go. Many will be injured, some might even die before the journey's end. Where are they going? Most probably to slaughter or to auction in Britain. But they could also be heading to somewhere in continental Europe, where they'll be slaughtered upon arrival after a journey that's lasted days. And if they're very young calves, they might be heading for a farm in France or Holland where solitary confinement in veal crates awaits them.

Did you know?
Every year, an estimated 185,000 lorryloads of hens are moved from farms to slaughterhouses in Britain.

The road to slaughter

►Why should animals have to suffer on their way to slaughter? Aren't there any laws to protect them at the end of their lives? One European Union law that came into force at the end of 1996 restricts the length of time calves, sheep and pigs can travel before they must be allowed to rest. But the allowed travelling times are far in excess of the maximum eight hours the RSPCA and many animal welfare researchers are calling for. Besides, there's a problem making the new laws stick. Different types of animals can be transported for between 20 and 30 hours at a time, with a one-hour food break in the middle. Then, if they haven't reached their destination, they must have a day's rest before the journey continues.

It's easy for drivers to fudge the truth about how long they've been travelling, and when the animals last got a break, when journeys are allowed to last for several days. Policing an eight-hour law, however, would be simple. Any animal carrier found more than an eight-hour drive away from its point of departure has obviously broken the law.

Did you know?
Each year Australia exports more than 5 million live sheep to the Middle East, and each year about 100,000 of them perish from heat stroke, starvation or disease on the journey. In 1996, the number of transport deaths rose dramatically when 67,488 sheep perished in a fire aboard the livestock carrier The Unice en route to Aquaba in Jordan.

It's not as if we don't know or care that millions of animals are being shipped about as if they were rolls of toilet paper or tinned peaches. All it takes to stir up public anger is a story on the evening news about live animal export. If anyone needs scientific proof that animals suffer in transport, there's plenty of it. Many researchers have found clear evidence that cramming animals into lorries and taking them on long journeys hurts them both physically and psychologically. The most stressful part of any journey is at the start when the animals are loaded into the lorry. Animals raised in factory farms see very few humans, and consequently are not used to being handled by humans. Suddenly, they find themselves being manhandled up ramps into a dark, alien environment full of animals they don't know. No wonder they're anxious and afraid.

Some animals cope better with the stresses of travel. When they're first loaded into an animal carrier, sheep's heart rates soared to more than twice their normal level. Yet after nine hours, their heart rates returned to normal. Pigs, however, don't fare so well. They're four times more likely to die than sheep during a journey.

Did you know?
One farmer stated in a BBC radio interview that she always tried to accustom her animals to the kinds of activities, sights and noises that they'd experience on the day they were transported to the slaughterhouse. Because her animals were already familiar with things like loading ramps, the stress they felt on the last day of their lives was considerably reduced.

❏ Pigs of a feather...

Pigs like to hang out in small groups and quickly become stressed when they're surrounded by lots of pigs they don't know. Researchers discovered that a stressed-out pig produces tough, dark meat. Not very appetizing. They also discovered that they could reduce the amount of stress pigs experience on their way to slaughter simply by keeping them together in the same small groups they lived in on the farm. This sounds like a kind thing to do, and it is. But it has an added bonus for pork eaters. Relaxed pigs produce tender meat. It's a clear case of how an animal benefits because it would also benefit us.

Virtual market

➤Since 1989 Scottish farmers have been able to sell their animals without a single one of them ever having to travel to market. They do it electronically, using an idea imported from Canada where distance can be a huge problem. Farmers enter information about their livestock into a mainframe computer to which buyers' personal computers are linked by modems. Buyers then bid against each other by telephone. Each buyer enters a bid on his computer and when he presses the return key the bid appears on everyone else's screen. The farmer can then send his animals directly to their final destination. It's not a perfect solution, but it cuts out one unnecessary trip for the animals.

What do you think?
Instead of trying to reduce travelling time or the stresses of travel, why don't we simply remove the torture of transport at the end of an animal's life by slaughtering it humanely where it has spent its life? Its chilled carcass can then be shipped to market. (New Zealand has been exporting its lamb frozen 'on the hook' like this instead of 'on the hoof' for years.) A change of attitude is needed to make this happen in Europe, where consumers, supermarkets and butchers insist that meat is fresh-killed. The Humane Slaughter Association's suggested solution is a mobile slaughterhouse. Can you think of any other solutions?

 CAUTION:
NOT FOR THE FAINT HEARTED

At the slaughterhouse

►Do you know what goes on in slaughterhouses, or abattoirs as they're also called? Farm animals are killed, yes, but do you know how? They're supposed to be slaughtered humanely. The actual wording of the regulations governing humane slaughter of farm animals says that animals must be 'rendered insensible to pain until death supervenes'. In other words, they should be stunned so that they feel no pain when they are strung up so that they can be bled to death by having their throats cut. Cattle are usually stunned by having a high-speed bolt driven into the brain, while pigs and most sheep are stunned by electric shock delivered by tongs pressed to each side of their heads. Chickens and turkeys are hung upside down by both legs and their heads are dipped into an electrified bath that stuns them.

You can imagine how difficult it must be to work in a slaughterhouse day after day, surrounded by terrified animals and the smells and sights of death. The ones who manage to stay in the job usually do it by hardening their hearts to the suffering going on around them, just like battlefield medics must do. The result is that many slaughterhouse workers often stop seeing the animals as living, aware creatures and instead look upon them as production units that must be processed if they are to meet their quota. And for every one who stays, there are probably several who leave after only a short time in the job. During their time on the slaughterhouse floor, these short-term workers lack the experience necessary to prevent animals from suffering. It takes knowledge and skill to properly stun an animal, and training to recognize when the job has not been done well. And it takes time to develop the skills and experience that are necessary to prevent animals suffering during the slaughtering process. How can a succession of inadequately trained people make sure that animals don't suffer in the assembly-line atmosphere of a modern slaughterhouse where all that counts is the number of animals that can be processed in an hour?

Did you know?
Research suggests that anoxia – or lack of oxygen – is a better way to stun animals, in particular chickens. Humans who have survived anoxia liken the sensation to feeling drunk. Anoxia could eliminate much of the stress felt by chickens before slaughter, because the birds could be stunned in their transport crates, sparing them the terrible final journey in shackles to the electric bath.

Each year millions of pigs and 90 per cent of all sheep are stunned by electric tongs to the sides of the head. An investigation by the Farm Animal Welfare Council (FAWC) discovered that slaughterhouse staff frequently don't know what voltage or current they should use, or how long they should apply the tongs. If the tongs are kept on for too short a time, which often seems to be the case, the animal can still feel pain while it's being shackled, hung and bled. FAWC has called for the use of head restraints for pigs, sheep and cattle so that the person using the electric tongs or stunning gun can apply them quickly and accurately to the correct parts of the head. Many animal welfare researchers are calling for more reliable and humane ways of slaughtering animals. For instance, it's possible to stop an animal's heart and stun its brain at the same moment by applying electrodes to its head and back so that a strong electrical current crosses the heart.

Stunning guns and electric tongs can work effectively on cattle, pigs and sheep – providing they're properly applied – but they're useless for chickens and turkeys. As many as 100,000 chickens might arrive at once at a slaughterhouse. They are removed by hand from their travelling crates and hung upside down on a moving belt that takes them to the electrified bath. When they emerge, stunned, from the water, their throats are cut, either by hand or machine. Next they're plunged into the scalding tank so that their feathers can be plucked easily. Unfortunately, most machines cut a bird's neck from behind and so might miss the main blood vessels at the front of the neck. This means that many birds are probably still alive and maybe even aware when they enter the scalding tank. But the production line moves so quickly, and so many birds go through in an hour, that staff have no time to check on the state of any individual bird. Turkeys go through the same process as chickens, but because their long wings hang below their heads, they often suffer more than chickens. Why? Before many turkeys have a chance of being stunned, they receive a very painful electric shock through their wingtips.

Did you know?
Researchers have invented a mechanical harvester, made up of soft rubber 'fingers' attached to rotors, which sweeps through a flock of broiler chickens, picks them up and places them on a conveyor belt for loading into crates for the journey to the slaughterhouse. Why a machine? Chickens that have seen very few people panic when farm workers handle them, resulting in many broken bones. But the rubber fingers don't faze them at all.

❏ Looking for kinder ways to kill

What goes on inside a sheep's brain after it has been stunned by electric tongs? To find out, researchers carried out experiments using the range of currents used in slaughterhouses. They discovered that stunning by electric tongs creates a type of electrical storm that sweeps across the brain and prevents it from being aware of what's going on around it. Applying the tongs correctly blocks all sensations of pain for up to nine minutes. However, because many animals are not stunned correctly in slaughterhouses, the researchers applied the tongs incorrectly and discovered that stunned sheep's brains sometimes had flashes of awareness as little as nine seconds after stunning. Unfortunately, the average amount of time between a sheep being stunned and having its throat cut is about 96 seconds. The researchers believe that the law should be rewritten so that animals must be made completely insensible by stunning, not just insensible to pain.

Tough new licensing standards for slaughterhouses were laid down in 1992 by the European Commission. Many slaughterhouses in Britain failed to achieve the required standards and were closed down. This wasn't necessarily all good news for British livestock. With fewer slaughterhouses available, the final journey for many animals is now much longer than it might previously have been. And the remaining slaughterhouses are under even greater pressure to process higher numbers of animals. When 100,000 broiler chickens arrive all at once and production lines speed up, what are a chicken's chances that it will go under the knife partially or wholly aware of pain? We know how to give animals a quick, painless death. But will we?

WHAT CAN YOU DO?

'It does not matter to an animal how we think but what we do.'
John Webster, Professor of Animal Husbandry, University of Bristol, 1994

The big question is do you decide that it's acceptable to eat animals so long as we take good care of them and make sure they don't suffer on our behalf? Or do you decide to become a vegetarian so that animals don't have to suffer in factory farms and be killed on your behalf? These are tough questions and many people are struggling with them. A quick look back at how the tradition of using animals came about might help you put a few things into perspective.

Our ancient ancestors first started domesticating animals about 10,000 years ago. Some animals, such as cattle, became symbols of personal wealth because they provided more than just meat and milk. They could work for us, carry our goods and pull our ploughs. Because of their ability to improve our standard of living, we cared more for them than we did for animals such as chickens or pigs that simply provided us with food. (An attitude that's carried through to the present day.) Regardless of how well we treated them as individuals, however, all domesticated animals made sure their species survived by allowing us to control how and where they live as well as how and when they die. If we had domesticated rhinos instead of pigs do you think they'd be threatened with extinction today?

Believe it or not!
The World Federation for the Protection of Animals estimates that, excluding poultry, as many as 1,000 million animals are killed each year for their meat.

There's a suggestion of a trade-off in what you've just read. This doesn't imply that pigs knocked on our ancient ancestor's door one day and said, 'Take us in and protect us, feed us, keep us warm in winter and make sure there's plenty of sun-block handy in summer, then, when we've had an easy, lazy life for a few years, you can eat us.' Or even that animals gave their tacit approval to being locked up in pens and controlled by humans. What it does imply is that survival comes first on everyone's agenda, whether you're a pig or a human. We found that putting our energies into domesticating animals had greater survival value than heading out at the icy crack of dawn and attempting to bring home the bacon with a sling-shot and a couple of mates. And if domesticating animals helped us, in some ways it also helped them. In the wild, the constant struggle to find food, to avoid being eaten, and to withstand extreme weather conditions often means a short, tough life followed by an agonizing death in the jaws of a predator, or a painful, lingering death from injury, starvation or disease. Very few wild animals die peacefully from old age in their own beds. Domestication promised someone else would supply the food, keep away the predators, provide shelter from the elements and maybe arrange for a quick death. In return for all these benefits, domesticated animals had to give up control of their own lives.

Did you know?
If you share the same eating habits as the average British citizen, in your lifetime you're likely to eat 550 poultry, 36 pigs, 36 sheep, 8 cattle, 10,000 eggs and dairy produce equivalent to 18 tonnes of milk!

It's easy to forget, surrounded as we are by all the clutter of high-tech living, that we belong to the animal kingdom. Lions, wolves and dogs are carnivores with digestive systems that specialize in processing chunks of unchewed meat. Deer, giraffes and horses are herbivores with digestive systems that make short work of vegetation. Bears, chimps and humans are omnivores with a history of eating just about anything as long as it's not too hard to digest. Humans overcame that problem and increased the menu that was available to them by learning to break down the tough stuff in plants by cooking them. That's the way we evolved – flexible and opportunistic – two of the secrets of our success.

What do you think?
Humans have been raising and killing animals for food for thousands of years. Yet today, with our knowledge of nutrition and agricultural science, we can feed ourselves very well on plants. Are we still justified in killing animals for food?

Are you like a bear?

►When you see film footage of a magnificent grizzly bear gorging itself on salmon it has snatched out of an Alaskan river, you don't recoil in horror and think, 'Why doesn't that cruel bear stick to eating berries?' You view it simply as a bear that sees an opportunity to grab a high protein, high energy meal and goes for it. With winter fast approaching, the bear can't afford to be too nice about its table manners. If it doesn't tuck away enough salmon each autumn it won't have adequate fat reserves to survive until spring, especially if it's a pregnant female.

Because we share with bears a long history of being berry-pickers-cum-predators and we see nothing wrong with bears killing to eat, many people assume that we have the same rights as the bear when it comes to killing and eating animals. But there's a difference between bears and humans. Bears don't sit around the camp-fire wondering whether it's wrong to inflict pain on a fish or deprive it of its life, because they are not moral beings. (Although there's some evidence that chimpanzees have laws and punish chimps that break them.)

Humans think about this kind of thing because we *are* moral beings, which gives us responsibilities towards each other, and towards other animals – responsibilities that they simply can't comprehend. A bear kills to survive, and it knows only one way to kill a salmon. Fish, we now know, feel pain when they're hooked on a fishing line. So they must feel considerable pain when they're crushed between the jaws of an enormous grizzly. Because a bear knows nothing about painless killing, however, it can't be considered cruel or immoral for the suffering it inflicts on the salmon. And therefore it's not responsible for its actions.

But humans do know how to alleviate suffering. We know what we must do to help farm animals live as good a life as they possibly can. We know what we must do to ensure that their deaths, and the hours that lead up to them, are as free from fear and pain as we can possibly make them. We know all these things, but do we choose to do them? Do we accept our moral responsibility? If we do, we might well decide that it's all right to kill and eat domestic animals providing we do everything possible to prevent them suffering on our behalf. You could, of course, use the same argument to claim that since we know how to survive without eating meat, we have a moral responsibility to become vegetarians and put an end to all animal suffering on our behalf.

> *The partnership deal our ancestors struck with the animals they domesticated so long ago has evolved into something hopelessly lopsided, with most of the benefits coming our way. Isn't it time we showed more respect and compassion for the animals that help us to survive?*

The vegetarian option

►Some people claim that the best thing you can do for farm animals is to stop eating all animal products and become a vegan. Others claim it's not necessary to go to this extreme. Just stop eating meat and become a vegetarian. People stop eating meat, eggs or dairy products for many reasons. Some do it for their health, others for their religion, and still others for their conscience because they cannot find it in their heart to be the cause of pain and suffering to animals. Some claim that becoming a vegan or vegetarian for this last reason is like giving up your right to vote. The people who have the most power to influence the governments are those who vote. Likewise, the people who can most influence the large corporations that have vested interests in factory farms are those who keep them in business by buying meat, eggs and dairy products and who therefore have the power to demand change.

This argument might work for people who have accepted that it's OK to kill and eat animals providing we take care of them properly. They might feel that big changes aren't going to happen overnight, so it's best to work from within the system to bring about gradual change. If enough people demand that supermarkets sell only meat, eggs and dairy produce that are produced humanely and refuse to buy products from factory farms, supermarkets would begin to look for alternative suppliers that could satisfy their customers' demands.

The argument won't work for people who have not accepted that it's OK to kill and eat animals, no matter how well we care for them. They'd argue that you don't have to eat animals to care about them and you can still campaign for animal welfare in farms whether or not you eat meat. Also, they'd claim, if less people eat meat, demand would drop and market opportunities for products from more humane, organic farms would rise. Of course, the ultimate argument from vegetarians is that if no one ate meat, no one would ever have to discuss the plight of animals in factory farms.

Organic farmers have their say

Not all farmers, however, operate factory farms. What do organic farmers have to say about the increasing interest in vegetarianism? They point out that unless you stop eating all animal products, you cannot claim that no animal is killed on your behalf. To produce milk, for example, a dairy cow must give birth to a calf, which is either slaughtered for meat a few months after it's born, or it's slaughtered almost immediately. And at the end of the dairy cow's much shortened life, she too is slaughtered and turned into mince or stewing beef. In a sustainable world, claim organic farmers, if you're not prepared to eat the unavoidable meat by-products of the dairy industry, you shouldn't drink milk.

> **Believe it or not!**
> You can walk for 47 minutes on the food energy contained in a chicken sandwich, but you'll be able to last 16 minutes longer on the energy contained in a peanut butter sandwich.

Organic farmers also point out that in factory farms animals eat grain, which people could eat, making this an inefficient use of natural resources. Organic farms, however, use natural resources wisely because their animals eat grass, which people can't eat. And an animal-free organic farm, which many vegans would like to see, is a contradiction in terms. Why? Because organic farming is sustainable agriculture based on the natural cycle of replacing nutrients taken out of the soil by plants with manure produced by plant-eating animals. If this cycle breaks down, the soil loses its fertility so that it can no longer support a wide diversity of plants, and it loses its structure so that it easily washes or blows away. All organic vegetables are grown in soil that's nurtured and held together by animal manure, not artificial fertilizers that can damage the environment. If you eat organic veggies, therefore, it doesn't make sense to talk about doing away with the animals that make them possible.

There are few easy questions, let alone answers, in this book. As you've just discovered, looking for ways to answer the simple black and white question, 'Will giving up eating meat help farm animals?', leads you to a maze of connections that colour it several shades of grey. The only advice this book can offer is that no matter what decision you arrive at, there is real value to be gained from supporting your own ideals, regardless of whether your personal actions bring about the change you'd like to see.

What do you think?
Is becoming a vegetarian or vegan the best way to stop animal suffering in factory farms?

The true value of beef cattle
A field used to graze beef cattle provides only ten per cent of the food it could provide if it were used to grow crops. Many people claim that this type of statistic proves there's no justification for keeping beef cattle, especially when there's so much hunger and poverty in the world. Yet not all pasture is fit for growing crops that we're willing to eat. And cattle and sheep are often kept on land that's considered more difficult to cultivate than other, more fertile, better drained or more accessible land.

Have you changed your mind?

It's time to turn back to those statements you considered at the beginning of this section and see if you've changed your mind about any of your responses. If you decide that becoming a vegetarian or vegan is the way you want to help reduce the suffering of animals in factory farms, all you have to do is stop eating animal products and make sure you know how to eat a balanced diet. Well, that's not quite all you should consider doing. Here are a few suggestions.

- Join an organization that campaigns for animal welfare (see pages 216-222) and do what you can to help them achieve their goals.
- Write to your local supermarket and ask them to supply free range eggs and meats from organic farms. Just because you no longer eat these products doesn't mean you can't influence their buying policy.
- Write to the Ministry of Agriculture (see page 218 for address) and ask for faster progress on animal welfare issues.
- If you're a vegetarian and feel very strongly about factory farms, tell people about them.

If you decide that you want to continue eating meat, eggs and dairy produce, providing we treat animals as humanely as possible, there are a number of actions you can take.

- Buy organically reared meat whenever possible, and look for free-range (or perchery/aviary/barn) eggs. Organic farming, with its reliance on traditional mixed farming techniques, is kinder to animals than intensive farming. But you must be prepared to pay a little more to ensure animal welfare.
- Ask for local products to reduce live transport of animals.
- Buy foods carrying the RSPCA Freedom Food symbol. If you can't find any Freedom Food products in your local supermarket, ask for them at the customer service desk. (If enough people ask for them, the store will start supplying them.)
- Write to your MP and the heads of as many

supermarket chains as possible asking what they're doing to improve animal welfare. Be sure to push for more organic and local foods and Freedom Food products in supermarkets. Consider getting signatures on a petition.

• Think about the kinds of meat you buy and how they are produced. For instance, chicken and pork come from the two systems of meat production that have the poorest animal welfare record, yet they're the most popular meats. And if you must eat veal, always ask for British 'welfare' veal (it's dark pink) instead of imported white veal because the calves it comes from aren't reared in crates or denied regular diets.

• Read Audrey Eyton's book, The Kind Food Guide and become a caring consumer.

• Too much protein and animal fat in your diet isn't good for you. So reduce the amount of meat, eggs and dairy products you eat, increase your intake of fruits, vegetables and whole grains and you'll feel healthier.

• Write to The Soil Association (address on page 219) and ask them to send you a copy of their list of suppliers of organic foods. (It costs £2.50.)

> 'The supermarkets now sell such a large proportion of all animal products that they can largely dictate the methods by which animals are farmed. They will supply precisely what you and I, their customers, desire, and they will know what we want by what we buy. It's as simple as that.'
> Audrey Eyton, The Kind Food Guide, 1991

How do you know it's organic?

►The word 'organic' is a legal definition and all products must be certified by a government-approved body, such as The Soil Association, which certifies about 70 per cent of all organic products in Britain. To carry The Soil Association Organic Standard symbol, all products must meet the Association's standards and each producer, processor or retailer displaying the symbol is inspected and registered yearly. Here are five organizations that have government approval to certify organic products:

The Soil Association
Organic Farmers & Growers Ltd.
Biodynamic Agricultural Association
Scottish Organic Producers
Irish Organic Farmers & Growers

Who sells organic food?

Supermarket	Fruit & veggies	Cereal products	Dairy products	Meat
Asda	✗	✗	✓✓✓	✗
Co-op	✓	✓	✓	✗
Safeway*	✓✓	✓✓	✓✓✓	✓
Sainsbury	✓✓	✓✓	✓✓✓	✓
Somerfield	✗	✗	✓	✗
Tesco	✓✓	✓✓	✓✓	✓
M&S	✗	✗	✗	✗
Waitrose	✓✓	✓✓	✓✓	✓

* = first supermarket to stock organic produce

107

Source: *The Soil Association Directory of Farm Shops, Box Schemes and Retailers, 1997*

Key: ✓✓✓= all stores   ✓✓= most stores
         ✓ = some stores   ✗= not stocked

❑ *Follow the freedom trail*
In 1994 the RSPCA, in response to what it saw as a growing demand for welfare-friendly food by the British public, launched the Freedom Food label. It's the RSPCA's guarantee that the animal who produces the food has been treated as humanely as possible and has enjoyed the Five Freedoms. When a farmer applies to join the Freedom Food scheme, the RSPCA investigates the welfare of his animals, as well as all the other links in the chain. For instance, if the farmer is an egg producer, the hatchery that supplies his laying hens, the hauliers who transport his chickens and the slaughterhouse that kills them must all meet the scheme's standards for animal welfare. Once accepted, members are monitored by spot checks.

(A few last words)

➤First a word for the farmers. They're not totally responsible for the way factory farms have turned out, and there must be many a farmer today who shakes his or her head in dismay when confronted with what intensive farming does to domestic animals. Also, centuries of farming tradition can blind us to animal cruelty, and many of the practices we now think of as cruel were once accepted without question.

When factory farming first became the accepted way to farm, no one foresaw all the problems it would cause for the environment. It was only much later that we realized how much contaminated slurry would be produced by pig farms. No one thought about the water pollution that would be caused by intensive dairy systems or the offensive smells that would arise from chicken sheds. And no one predicted that feeding high protein fish meal to chickens would result in extensive damage to the seabed and the depletion of fish stocks.

Not all farmers, of course, operate intensive systems that are harmful to both animals and the environment. And the number of farmers who use organic methods – for instance, avoiding hormone and antibiotic treatments as a matter of course or employing environmentally-friendly (and more animal-friendly) traditional mixed farming techniques – is steadily growing in response to increased demand. Currently, 0.3 per cent of all farms in the UK are organic, while several other European countries are aiming for 10 per cent by the millennium. Austria currently sets the pace with 12 per cent of all its farms using organic farming methods.

The government sets the agricultural policy of the nation, not the farmer, and it's the government that must find answers to four large problems:

1 How to balance out supply and demand.
2 How to give farm animals as fulfilling a life as possible.
3 How to farm in harmony with the environment.
4 How to ensure farmers can earn a decent living while doing everything they can for the welfare of their animals and for the environment.

You can help focus the government on this task by writing to the Minister of Agriculture, Fisheries and Food (see page 218 for address). Just as you can help focus supermarkets on the need to change their suppliers by demanding more organic foods. To begin with, you'll have to be prepared to pay a little extra for them. But the greater the demand, the faster the supply will grow. And when the supply is large enough, prices will tumble.

❏ Seeing through Daisy's eyes

An American woman called Temple Grandin wanted to understand what a farmyard was like from a cow's point of view. She had struggled all her life to come to terms with autism and believed that her disability made it possible for her to empathize with animals. For instance, she could tell at 50 m whether a cow was afraid. After spending plenty of time with cows, one of the things she discovered was that they were terrified by shadows and bright spots of light that people didn't even notice. Temple went on to become one of the leading US designers of agricultural equipment – equipment that's designed with an animal's needs in mind.

> 'For 3 pence per person per week we can free chickens and pigs from the misery of factory farms.'
> Peter Stevenson, Compassion in World Farming, BBC TV interview, 18 September 1997

QUIZ

True or false?

How much do you really know about the food business? Try your hand at this true or false quiz to find out.

1 True ☐ **False** ☐ In the UK, what farmers can grow and how they can grow it is limited by the country's four or five biggest supermarkets.

2 True ☐ **False** ☐ British taxpayers pay approximately £145 million a year just to get rid of the nitrates and pesticides that find their way into drinking water from intensive farming systems.

3 True ☐ **False** ☐ Every year, an area of the world almost as large as the British Isles becomes infertile.

4 True ☐ **False** ☐ British supermarkets currently import as much as 70 per cent of the organic produce they sell.

5 True ☐ **False** ☐ The market for organic produce in British supermarkets is predicted to grow from around 1 per cent of sales today to 5 per cent by the millennium.

6 True ☐ **False** ☐ More than 40 per cent of the world's grain is fed to animals.

7 True ☐ **False** ☐ Intensive farming of pigs and cattle pollutes rivers and destroys their wildlife.

8 True ☐ **False** ☐ A Gallup poll conducted in 1968 showed that, even then, farmers were as opposed to factory farming methods as most other people were.

(Answers page 223)

=Section Three=

RESEARCH LABORATORIES

*'The things that get done to the animals here
are infinitely nicer than what happens in your
average factory farm or abattoir.'*
Researcher who wished to remain anonymous

In April 1990, the animal rights organization Advocates for Animals wrapped up a two-year undercover investigation into the work of a distinguished British scientist. The government inquiry that followed the release of its findings resulted in both the scientist and his assistant losing their licence to experiment on animals. Others who were also responsible for the animals in his laboratory were severely reprimanded. What gruesome acts had the scientist performed to merit the ban? Mostly acts of incompetence. He was 89 years old, his memory and eyesight were failing and he had difficulty handling medical and surgical equipment.

No doubt the scientist's intentions were honourable enough. He was researching the causes of excess sugar in the blood, which he thought might shed new light on the treatment of diabetes. (Although insulin was discovered many years ago and is a life-saver, some diabetics still develop severe complications later in life.) But his methods were highly questionable. One of his experiments involved heating the shaved abdomen of a rabbit with a lamp to see what effect heat had on blood sugar levels. Because of the scientist's lapses of memory, animals often suffered through painful procedures with too little anaesthetic. And his poor eyesight and clumsiness with a syringe meant that he bungled many attempts at injecting anaesthetic into veins.

> *A rabbit lies spread-eagled with its limbs tied to a table. An anglepoise lamp sits only centimetres above its exposed, shaved abdomen. The heat from the lamp is intense. The rabbit jumps. Later, as its skin begins to scorch, there is a faint smell of cooking.*

The terrible irony of this sad tale is that if the scientist had kept up-to-date with what other scientists were doing, he would have discovered that many of his experiments were unnecessary. The answers he was seeking had already been found. How could this type of incompetent and inhumane experiment be allowed to happen in a country that prides itself on both the standard of its scientific work and its concern for animals? Everyone involved seemed to turn a blind eye to what the scientist was doing. And instead of halting his work, inspectors from the Home Office – who visited his laboratory many times during the two years the experiments were being conducted – merely suggested that he use rabbits instead of cats and give them 'terminal anaesthesia' to make sure they never woke up again. Why was he allowed to continue? Possibly because the man had enjoyed a distinguished career and no one wanted to be the one to force him to retire. The only ones to suffer under this blanket of silence were some defenceless rabbits. And they weren't about to tell anybody.

The battle between animal rights groups and scientists who experiment on animals – or vivisectionists as some prefer to call them – has been raging for many years. Vivisection is the practice of cutting up live animals in the quest for scientific knowledge, and it's been around since the time of ancient Greece. Today, we use it as a label to describe any experiment that causes a living animal to suffer. In Britain it is against the law to cause *unnecessary* suffering to animals. So how can scientists get away with making animals suffer in the name of science? Presumably, because it's seen as *necessary* suffering.

❑ Only competent people need apply

In 1876, Britain became the first country to pass a law controlling the use of animals in laboratories. In 1986, it was replaced by the Animals (Scientific Procedures) Act. The Act states that only competent people are allowed to conduct research and that animals must be looked after properly. Researchers must be able to prove to the Home Secretary that any distress they are likely to cause to animals is well justified by the likely benefits of their research. In addition, they must design their experiments so they use as few animals as possible. They must use non-animal alternatives wherever possible. And above all, they must keep animal suffering to a minimum with the use of painkillers or anaesthetics. If they do all of these things, they won't be prosecuted for cruelty to animals.

In 1996 there were more than 2.7 million scientific procedures (this includes everything from taking blood samples to infecting animals with fatal diseases) on animals in Britain. Most were for medical research or to test whether products work well or are safe to use. Worldwide, researchers use an estimated 100 million animals in laboratories every year.

There are no simple answers to be found in the debate between vivisectionists and anti-vivisectionists, especially when not all anti-vivisectionists share the same point of view. Some believe that animals should never be experimented on, regardless of how much we might benefit from the results of the experiments. Others believe that the issue is too complex to make such a sweeping statement. They share with many vivisectionists the belief that in some cases the benefit to humans far outweighs the suffering to animals and so justifies using animals in experiments, providing we treat them with respect and compassion and do everything possible to alleviate their pain.

What's your opinion?
It's time to make some tough decisions again. If you can't make up your mind, just tick off 'I'm not sure', then come back to this spot later.

Any animal experimentation is wrong if it causes suffering.
I agree ☐   I disagree ☐   I'm not sure   ☐
Making animals suffer to keep us supplied with 'new and improved' products is wrong.
I agree ☐   I disagree ☐   I'm not sure   ☐
We should continue using animals in medical research because the benefits to us outweigh the costs to them.
I agree ☐   I disagree ☐   I'm not sure   ☐
We can reduce animal suffering by changing our lifestyle and our expectations.
I agree ☐   I disagree ☐   I'm not sure   ☐

What supporters of animal research say:
- Many important medical breakthroughs depended on animal research.
- Alternatives to animal experimentation can give incomplete results.
- For every rat used in medical research, ten are exterminated outside the laboratory as pests.
- Animal research is necessary to develop treatments for many serious diseases.
- However much we care about animals, human health and safety come first.

What critics of animal research say:
- The fact that animals would choose not to suffer if they could is reason enough to stop hurting them.
- Researchers have plenty of alternatives they can use besides animals.
- It's unfair to use animals to test hundreds of new products each year that we don't need. Animal experiments have held back medical progress because they are misleading.
- Whether the outcome of an experiment is a cure for cancer or a new lipstick, animals suffer.

If we didn't rear animals in factory farms and kill them so that we can eat their flesh and wear their skins, use them as entertainment, exterminate them because they're a nuisance, or hunt them for sport, the ethics of using animals in experiments for our own gain wouldn't be debatable. The act of inflicting pain on small, helpless creatures when and how we feel like it would be seen as an act of bullying, which is contemptible. But we do kill animals and eat them, we do use them as entertainment, we do exterminate them as pests and we do hunt them for sport.

If you think it's acceptable to do any of these things, then it's logical to think that it might also be acceptable to use animals in research. But logic and emotions don't necessarily go hand in hand and that's what makes the debate about vivisection so difficult. It's not easy to hear the hard facts about what is done to animals in laboratories and not feel revolted, even if you do agree that since you're prepared to eat meat, wear leather shoes or put a piece of cheese in a mousetrap you should also be prepared to use animals in research.

EXPERIMENTS TO MAKE US FEEL BETTER

'There is no humane person who believes that we are free to use animals as we will, just because the goal is knowledge. But there are many who argue that experiments on live animals are ... necessary for the advance of science, and of medical science in particular.'
Roger Scruton, philosopher

When you're sick you visit the doctor and come home with a prescription for some kind of medicine. The law requires that all new medicines must be tested on animals before they can be given to humans. But did you know that your medicine might have been tested on as many as 1,000 animals? The most likely testers of your prescription drug would have been mice or rats. Ever wonder why so many mice and rats are used in medical research? It's not because their insides are put together like ours — pigs are much more like us than rats — or because they react to chemicals like us, it's because they're small, easy to handle, cheap to buy and they rapidly produce lots of babies.

Of course, not all medical research is carried out on mice and rats. Rabbits, ferrets, cats, dogs, pigs, cows, monkeys, birds, reptiles, amphibians and fish all play their part so that we can lead healthier lives. And not all medical research ends up benefiting only humans. Animals suffer from similar types of diseases to us, so medical research has given us the ability to successfully treat animals too.

The main arguments put forward by anti-vivisectionists for not using animals in medical research, apart from the suffering it causes, are that animals don't get exactly the same illnesses we do (for instance, they develop different types of cancer and heart disease), their bodies don't work quite like ours, and they sometimes react to drugs differently from us. All these differences, they claim, means that the results of experiments on animals can at best be unreliable and at worst downright dangerous.

Take a closer look at the medicine you hope will cure what ails you, and you'll find that things aren't as straightforward as you'd wish. Medicines are powerful drugs, sometimes too powerful for our bodies to handle. Making sure that medicines do what they're supposed to do without horrible side-effects is a vital part of medical research. And it's a part that has given animal rights supporters enough ammunition to shoot holes in the argument that animal-based research is reliable. Drugs that have no harmful effect on animals have proven dangerous to people, even killing them, and vice versa. For example, the heart drug Eraldin was tested on mice, rats, dogs, even monkeys and no bad reactions to the drug surfaced. Yet 7,000 human patients developed serious medical conditions, including damage to their sight and hearing. Some went blind and 23 died. Meanwhile, across-the-counter drugs such as Aspirin and Paracetamol, which are very effective in getting rid of human aches, pains and fever, can poison the family cat. And, as anti-vivisectionists are fond of pointing out, penicillin, which was hailed as one of the greatest medical breakthroughs ever, can prove deadly to guinea pigs. Yes, it is true that penicillin can kill guinea pigs, but only in doses big enough to stop a bull in its tracks. When the dose given to guinea pigs was worked out according to their weight, in the same way as yours is, they showed no harmful side-effects whatsoever! You can see some of the traps you can fall into in this debate.

'Either the animal is not like us, in which case there is no reason for performing the experiment; or else the animal is like us, in which case we ought not to perform on the animal an experiment that would be considered outrageous if performed on one of us.'
Peter Singer, philosopher

Why do scientists believe that animal experimentation gives reliable results? They claim that because rats, mice, cats, dogs, monkeys and humans are all mammals and we're all descended from common ancestors, we're biologically very similar. Occasionally, they'll come across a result in one species that doesn't match the result in another, but they feel they can learn from differences in results as well as similarities. Furthermore, they claim that without all the work that has been done with animals, many of the breakthroughs in 20th-century medicine might still be waiting to happen.

If you were a research scientist on the brink of discovering a new treatment for a fatal disease, and the only experiments likely to provide the answers inflict suffering on animals, what would you do?

Scientists are aware of the danger of relying strictly on animal testing. And so is the law. Developing, testing and licensing a new medicine is a lengthy, expensive process and animals are normally used at only one stage. First the medicine must be tested in the laboratory on human tissues, backed up if possible by the use of computer models. (See page 150.) If the results look good, the medicine is tested on animals to see what happens in a living system. After the medicine passes the animal test, it must be tested on healthy human volunteers – often scientists, doctors and medical students. If they don't experience harmful side-effects, the medicine is given to a small group of volunteer patients who are suffering from the disease the medicine is intended to treat. If the medicine helps these patients without any nasty side-effects, doctors in other hospitals offer the treatment to any of their patients who want to take part in lengthy clinical trials. These can last for several years and involve data from thousands of patients. If at any time harmful side-effects are reported, doctors stop the tests. If not, the medicine is licensed for sale and family doctors can prescribe it. As you can see, not all the testing for a new medicine involves animals, but they play a vital role in its safe development. Vivisectionists can rattle off a long list of drugs that animal research helped bring about such as:

1920s	Insulin for diabetics
1930s	Modern anaesthetics, Diphtheria vaccine
1940s	Penicillin, whooping cough vaccine
1950s	Polio vaccine, drugs for high blood pressure
1960s	Drugs for mental illness
1970s	Drugs for ulcers, asthma and leukaemia
1980s	Drugs for viral diseases and transplants
1990s	Meningitis vaccine

According to anti-vivisectionists, however, scientists seem to forget that animal research wasn't solely responsible for the discovery of all these drugs. Many of them, including penicillin and the early anaesthetics, were discovered either through careful observation of human patients or by chance. And the differences between human and animal body systems and reactions meant that not all the results were as reliable as they should have been.

For instance, one of the most popular drugs for treating high blood pressure, Propanolol, had no effect on the blood pressure of any of the animals on which it was tested. It was only when it was given to human patients as a treatment for a painful heart condition called angina that its blood-pressure-lowering ability was discovered. And researchers worked for decades to discover a drug that would stop a patient's body from rejecting a transplanted organ. Finally, after an estimated 500,000 animals in Britain alone gave up their lives in transplant experiments, Cyclosporin A was discovered. It tested well in animals, but caused high blood pressure and kidney failure in many human patients.

Did you know?
Experiments with rats have revealed how much exercise can help stroke victims regain the use of their limbs. Too much, too soon, can double the amount of injury to the brain.

What do you think?
Human organs for transplantation are in short supply. So medical researchers have been breeding genetically engineered pigs that possess a human gene in the hope that it will make its organs less likely to be rejected by a human body. It's unlikely that any human will receive a pig's heart in the near future, however, because of the danger of transferring potentially lethal viruses from pigs to humans. We breed pigs to eat; are we right to breed them so that we can harvest their organs?

> '*Some people say that animal experimentation has failed because it has not given us cures for the diseases facing our society. It would be just as fair to say that studying cells in the laboratory or patients who attend hospitals has failed for the same reason.*'
> **Research for Health Charities Group**

Researchers use animals as stand-ins for human beings for several reasons. They help them develop better treatments, medicines and vaccines, improve their surgical techniques and find other ways to prevent diseases. For instance, dogs played a role in developing modern anaesthetics because their hearts, lungs and chest cavities are similar to those of human adults, while pigs were used to research bed sores and ulcers because their skin is so like ours.

Whatever human disease researchers are trying to conquer, they first try to produce its symptoms in a laboratory animal. If the disease is tooth decay, for example, the animal is fed a high-sugar diet until its teeth begin to rot. Researchers can then test experimental vaccines to see if they halt tooth decay. Next time you visit the dentist you should say a silent thank you to the animals who helped eliminate many painful procedures from dentistry. If the disease is cancer, the animal is given cancer either by transplanting tumours into its body, exposing it to radiation or injecting it with cancer-causing viruses or chemicals. The animal is then either used to test new anti-cancer drugs or it is studied to give information on how the disease progresses, then it is killed so that an autopsy can provide even more information.

> *'When experiments can be brought under the heading 'medical' we are inclined to think that any suffering they involve must be justifiable because the research is contributing to the alleviation of suffering. But ... the testing of therapeutic drugs is less likely to be motivated by the desire for maximum good to all than by the desire for maximum profit.'*
> *Peter Singer, Philosopher*

You've no doubt seen photos of unfortunate mice with cancerous tumours larger than their heads. While many people might be willing to sacrifice mice to find a cure for cancer, it's hard to confront the reality of their suffering without asking, 'Isn't there another way?' Animal rights supporters say 'Yes!' (see pages 144-152) but animal researchers say 'Not anything as reliable.' Why? Drugs are powerful chemicals that don't just affect the part of the body that needs treatment. They affect the entire body. So even though preliminary research can be done using donated human tissue, to get the full picture tests have to be carried out on an entire living body.

❑ Who to thank?

People who support animal-based medical research point to the list of medical breakthroughs – things like life-support systems for premature babies, artificial heart valves, coronary bypass operations, antibiotics, vaccines, treatment for asthma, hip replacement surgery, CAT scanning for better diagnosis – and claim that animal experimentation is largely responsible for our improved health today.

Animal rights supporters, meanwhile, are quick to point out that the reason we're so much healthier than our great-great-grandparents ever were is thanks to improved sanitation, housing, nutrition and education. Quite right, respond animal researchers, but who did the research on nutrition that told us what we should be eating to improve our health? They agree that an efficient sewage system eliminates the danger of cholera and typhoid, that a good diet builds a strong body better able to fight off disease, that living in uncrowded conditions reduces the risk of TB and that education helps us understand the need for good hygiene and a healthy lifestyle. But they claim that all these advances in public health don't make you immune to disease when it strikes. If they did millions of people wouldn't die from global outbreaks of influenza. And five million people worldwide wouldn't have died from the Aids virus. That's why they insist that improvements in public health must go hand in hand with advances in medicine. And many of those advances depend on animals at one time or another during their development. To which animal rights supporters might reply, 'Show us the cure for influenza and Aids and we might listen.'

Believe it or not!
Mice are so adaptable, they've even been found in the bottom of mines, inside the rim of extinct volcanoes and in the middle of deserts.

The need for the body test to react in as similar a way as possible to a human body has led scientists to alter the genetic make-up of laboratory animals, mice in particular. For example, in 1992 a group of scientists in Edinburgh succeeded in breeding mice that had a faulty gene that made them develop the mouse version of cystic fibrosis (CF), a killer disease that affects young people. First they used these genetically altered mice to test possible treatments for the disease. Then they found a way to remove the defective gene that causes the disease in mice and replace it with a normal one, which produced a vital protein missing in CF sufferers. This wasn't necessarily good news for the mice, but it gave fresh hope to 6,000 young people in Britain that a cure might be around one of the corners.

What do you think?
Are we right to inflict terrible diseases on laboratory animals if in doing so we can save human lives? Would your answer change if you or someone you loved suffered from CF or cancer or Aids?

In the future, you'll hear a lot about 'transgenic' animals – animals that carry genes from two different species. For instance, sheep + goat = geep (or shoat if you wish). What do transgenic animals have to offer medical research? Scientists hope that transgenic animals will be able to produce useful human antibodies, vaccines or hormones in their blood or milk. British scientists have already produced Rosie the cow. Rosie looks like a cow, walks like a cow and moos like a cow. By any definition, she's a cow. Yet the cells in her body contain a tiny fragment of human DNA – the one responsible for producing milk. That's right, Rosie the cow makes human milk and may save the lives of premature human babies, who are born long before their mothers are able to produce milk.

The same scientists have also reported rearing cows and sheep whose milk contains the key proteins and antibodies found in human blood plasma – the colourless liquid that's left when red haemoglobin is removed from blood. They hope one day to be able to create a steady supply of blood plasma for use in surgery and transfusions simply by milking cows and sheep. The technique used to create human blood plasma in animal milk may also be able to create animal milk that contains natural human antibodies against diseases such as CF, haemophilia, osteoporosis and certain cancers. Are we right to tinker with animals in this way, even if retrieving the substances needed for treatments causes them no pain? Isn't there a much bigger picture here that we're ignoring – our arrogant belief that animals and everything in the world were made for our benefit?

> *'30,000 annual heart disease fatalities could be averted if people ate more fruit and vegetables.'*
> **Andrew Tyler, Director of Animal Aid**

What do you think?
Since 1990, the number of animals bred with harmful genetic defects (for example, mice with cancer-producing genes) has doubled, while the number of genetically engineered transgenics (such as geeps) has increased sixfold. Should we be worried by this trend?

Milestones in medical knowledge

17th century: At last, the mystery of how the blood circulates and how the lungs work is solved.

18th century: We learn how to measure blood pressure.

19th century: Vaccination gives us immunity to disease for the first time.

1900s: We discover antibodies (proteins made by white blood cells that attack foreign invaders) and how our hormone system works.

1920s: We realize what vitamins are and discover that bacteria can be altered by DNA transfer.

1930s: The workings of the nervous system become clear, and we discover tumour viruses.

1940s: We understand how embryos develop.

1950s: How muscles contract and how we create energy from food are finally understood.

1960s: Light is shed upon how the eye, ear and liver work.

1970s: We understand transplantation antigens (substances thought of as foreign by the body and which trigger an immune response) and discover prostaglandins (cause smooth muscle contraction) and monoclonal antibodies (proteins that can be designed to recognize and stick to cancer cells).

1980s: Transgenic animals (genetically engineered animals that contain genes from two species) become a reality, the way our immune systems react to foreign grafts and virus-infected cells becomes clear and we discover that Aids is a viral disease.

1990s: We discover how the brain functions and malfunctions and what causes inherited disease.

On 4 March 1998, PPL Therapeutics – the same British laboratory that cloned Dolly the sheep – announced they can now produce enough blood clotting Factor IX in sheep's milk to treat all the haemophiliacs (people who can easily bleed to death because their blood cannot clot) in the world.

EXPERIMENTS TO MAKE US SAFER AND SMARTER

> *'Animal experimentation will one day be judged a crime.'*
> Leonardo da Vinci

Have you ever counted all the cleaning or personal hygiene products in your home? Make a list of them. You'll be astonished at how many there are. Every one of them is made up of several ingredients. And the law requires that each one of those ingredients is tested to find out whether it's harmful when swallowed or when it comes in contact with skin or eyes. And the usual way to do that is to test it on animals. Aha! you might quickly respond. I'm careful to buy only products that haven't been tested on animals. Quite right, too. But even though a finished product might have been tested on human volunteers, this in itself is no guarantee that its *ingredients* weren't tested on animals at some time in the past.

Many people believe that all animal experiments have to do with medical research, but that's not so. Of the 2,716,587 scientific procedures carried out on animals in the UK in 1996 (up 7,000 on the year before), more than half a million were to research and develop new drugs. Cancer and immunology research used another half million animals. When you add in a further million for other types of medical research and basic biological research – done to improve our knowledge of how things work, which can help in the development of better treatments – you've accounted for roughly 75 per cent of the total procedures.

So what kind of procedures make up the remaining 25 per cent? Many of them test non-medical substances such as household products, food additives, alcohol, tobacco, cosmetics, toiletries and agricultural chemicals on animals to see if they're irritating or poisonous. Others attempt to increase agricultural productivity by creating 'super animals' for the farm, or find out why humans behave the way they do, or test the effects of new weapons or teach biology and anatomy to university students. Here's a look at what happens in these tests.

> '*We must make the public realize the extent to which their lives depend on animal experiments.*'
> *Colin Blakemore, Professor of Physiology*

Tests that do more than irritate

►Rabbits must be very sensitive creatures because they're considered ideal for tests that discover whether new ingredients are irritating to sensitive parts of the body such as eyes and skin. The real reason rabbits are used more than any other animal is because they're docile creatures who are easy to handle. But if any animal were tailor-made for eye tests, it's the unfortunate rabbit, because it can't produce tears to wash away irritating substances and so ruin the experiment. If any new ingredients are used in shampoos, washing powders, paints, weed-killers, dyes, cleaning fluids – anything we use that might create problems if it splashes in our eyes and makes contact with our skin – they must be tested on rabbits. How? During an eye irritancy test, rabbits are restrained so they can't scratch their heads, then a substance is either dripped or sprayed into one of their eyes. This could be anything from a detergent to an industrial chemical. (If you've ever got shampoo in your eye you have a slight idea how painful this must be.) No pain relief is given.

At the end of the test, which might last for days, the rabbits' eyes are examined for damage ranging from slight irritation to blindness. During a skin irritancy test, rabbits are restrained so they can't lick themselves, then they are shaved and the test substance is applied to a patch of skin. Often the skin is scratched first. Cosmetics, skin creams, weed-killers and pesticides are tested this way. These tests are known as the Draize eye and skin irritancy tests, named after J.H. Draize, the person who developed the scales against which all tests results are checked. (The scales measure physical changes to the eye or the skin, not suffering.)

There has been such an understandable outcry about the cruelty of the Draize tests that researchers are trying to develop alternative ones that don't involve animals. Animal rights supporters point out that not only are these tests cruel, but they are also unreliable because animals don't always react to substances as we would. They report that rats, for instance, absorb substances through their skin five times faster than we do, while rabbits are less varied in their response to skin irritancy tests than humans are, and react more strongly than we do to mild or moderate irritants.

Q. Are you opposed to testing cosmetics and toiletries on animals? Yes ☐ No ☐

Q. Do you think that household products should be tested on animals? Yes ☐ No ☐

A. If you said yes to the first question, you agree with 96 per cent of people who responded to a 1993 RSPCA survey. If you said no to the second question, you agree with 95 per cent of people who responded in the same survey.

These tests are lethal

➤If you wanted to find out whether a new product was poisonous, how would you go about it? The traditional way is to carry out a Lethal Dose 50 per cent test (usually shortened to LD50). This involves force-feeding a substance to a group of animals to discover at what dosage 50 per cent of them die. Forcing food additives, new medicines, toothpaste, insecticides or fertilizers down animals' throats is a crude and inhumane way to test for poisonous substances. If more than 50 per cent of the test group survives being force-fed a certain amount of a new substance, a second group of animals is given a larger dose. This continues with different groups until 50 per cent of one group die. Before dying, animals can suffer vomiting, convulsions, internal bleeding and paralysis. There have even been reports of the dose becoming so large that the animals died instead from ruptured stomachs.

> '*In 1984 the CTPA Council issued a statement urging its member companies to press their suppliers of ingredients to carry out 'limit' tests rather than LD50 tests, to establish safety.*'
> **Cosmetic, Toiletry & Perfumery Association**

Most scientists agree that the LD50 test is far too crude to give any meaningful results and welcomed the changes made to EC legislation in 1989 which accepted an alternative test, called the Fixed Dose Procedure, or limit test, in its place. This test uses far fewer animals and its purpose isn't to poison animals until they die, but only until they show visible signs of poisoning. This distinction might not mean too much to a mouse, rat, rabbit or dog that's just been poisoned, but it's a small step in the right direction.

Did you know?
About 720,000 animals took part in tests in 1996 to find out whether new substances were harmful. Of these, 181,000 were poisoned to death with lethal doses (many of these were involved in drug research). And cosmetic testing increased by about 30 per cent from the previous year for a total of 2,800 procedures.

These tests are cancerous

▶Some rats and mice spend their lives eating controlled doses of test substances to find out if they cause cancer. According to animal rights supporters, many of the animals used in these feeding tests are not in the best of health. This might strike you as being a slightly ludicrous expectation, given their steady diet of carcinogenic substances, but laboratories pride themselves on the care they take of their animals. The majority of laboratory animals are in excellent shape (at least at the start of an experiment) but these rodents are frequently overweight and are often highly inbred. This means that they're all too closely related. When close relatives mate, any genetic defects found in both parents have a greater chance of surfacing in their offspring. The genetic defects in some strains of laboratory mice make them prone to developing cancer. Up to 80 per cent of them will grow tumours regardless of what they eat. If everything the animal rights supporters claim is true, this is hardly a reliable test and the ethics of continuing to breed mice that are genetically predisposed to develop cancer are highly questionable.

These tests create super animals

➤First we invented the factory farm, now we're trying to create super animals to live in them. But not everyone is happy with this type of experimentation. In the US, for instance, scientists have had to return to the drawing-board after producing a genetically-engineered 'superpig' designed to grow faster than normal and so make a bigger profit for the farmer. What went wrong? The superpigs grew fast enough, but they became stressed out and suffered from arthritis, weak muscles and poor eyesight. Other types of research try to find drugs that will prevent animals developing 'vices' such as tail-gnawing in pigs or feather-pecking in chickens, both animals kept in overcrowded conditions in factory farms.

What do you think?
Does it strike you as odd that while farmers were being told to reduce yields because of food surpluses, agricultural researchers were working hard to find ways of making animals grow bigger or produce more milk or eggs or wool? Shouldn't they concentrate now on how to produce food in more humane ways?

Q. Are you concerned by our ability to genetically alter crops and animals that we use as food?
Yes ☐   No ☐

A. If you said yes, you agree with 68 per cent of the people who took part in a 1997 Gallup poll on behalf of the *Daily Telegraph*.

Is this any way to behave?

➤Scientists who are trying to unravel how the human brain works and why we behave the way we do, often study animals. All mammals, including you, have brains that are made up of the same kinds of cells. They function in similar ways and they contain the same basic structures. The hope is that animals with similar brains to ours will be able to provide some answers to the many questions that still remain. One way of doing this is to implant electrodes in an animal's brain to be able to see what happens inside it when the animal is exposed to such things as pain, hunger, loneliness, complete darkness or objects that cause fear or recognition. The researcher can then match up behaviours with brain activity.

In 1986, for instance, monkeys with electrodes implanted in their brains were restrained in chairs at Oxford University while researchers showed them different images on a TV and recorded the reactions of individual brain cells to each picture. In a similar experiment the following year, five sheep were suspended in a hammock in front of a slide projector so that the reaction of certain cells in their brains to friendly and menacing faces could be recorded. They found that one type of cell reacted to sheep with big horns, another responded to familiar looking sheep and a third reacted when pictures of dogs, pigs and people were projected. A second way of finding out how the brain affects behaviour is to damage a specific part of an animal's brain then watch what happens. In one famous experiment, a researcher removed a small part of a rat's brain that controls fear. The by now fearless rat walked straight up to a cat and started nibbling on its ear!

What do you think?
Do these kinds of experiments really help us understand how the human brain works and why we behave the way we do? Many scientists claim that animal studies have provided much valuable insight into human brain function and behaviour and they can continue to do so. Animal rights supporters, however, disagree. They claim that all these experiments show is how animal brains work and why animals behave the way they do. So do we really need to continue experimenting on animals?

❏ The eyes have it

In 1985 several two-day-old rhesus monkeys each had one of their eyes permanently sewn shut. (Another group didn't have one of their eyes sewn shut until they were 18 months old.) Over a period of five years, the monkeys were killed and their brains were examined to see if any changes had happened in the parts of the brain that handle vision. The brains of the monkeys who had been able to see normally for 18 months before having one eyelid closed showed no changes. But the brains of the monkeys who had been deprived of the sight in one eye practically since birth, showed definite changes. What experiments like this confirmed was that human infants should not have operations that require one or both eyes to be bandaged for any length of time before the vision centres in their brains are fully developed, otherwise they lose the ability to see out of whichever eye has been bandaged.

All you want to know about killing

►Each year in Britain several thousand animals are killed by 'friendly fire' – which includes bullets, gas, fire, infection and irradiation – in weapons research designed to provide better protection for troops and improve treatment for casualties. It makes no difference to monkeys shot through the head with ball bearings, or sheep and pigs gunned down by high-velocity rifles that they were anaesthetized when it happened, or that it was the friendly side doing the shooting and not the enemy, they still end up dead. Some, however, aren't allowed to die until new ideas for treatments can be tried on their wounds. No one likes to think of defenceless animals being used as target practice for a new Ministry of Defence weapon. Or being exposed to nerve gas, radiation, deadly viruses or any of the terrible weapons now used in modern warfare. But when given a straight choice between testing weapons on animals or testing them on humans, do you not think most people would choose animals?

What do you think?
Rather than worrying about whether it's preferable to test new weapons on animals or people, shouldn't we instead be worrying about why we continue to create ever more destructive weapons?

Are all these experiments necessary?

►There are four basic reasons why animal research is done:

1 To test the claims of new products, e.g. medicines, veterinary products, cosmetics or toiletries.

2 To find out whether new products are harmful when swallowed (or breathed in) or when they come in contact with skin or eyes, e.g. household cleaners, toiletries, cosmetics, medicines, veterinary products, pesticides.

3 To act as stand-ins for human beings in medical research, e.g. in development of new medicines, vaccines, surgical techniques and treatments, developing better ways of diagnosing diseases and studying genetic diseases.

4 To act as stand-ins for human beings in basic biological research so that we can learn more about how body systems and organs work, e.g. knowing how healthy bodies work and what happens to them when injury or disease strikes is the first crucial step to developing treatments.

Some of the experiments on this list are required by law. For instance, new drugs must be tested on animals before being tested on humans. Most animal experiments, however, are not required by law. Many of them are done to prevent major corporations being sued in the event that something goes wrong.

Some images of the way we use animals doubtless send shivers down your spine. Defenceless animals being used as target practice by the Ministry of Defence, or having electrodes inserted into their brains so that we can see how they work, or being force-fed a new medicine or lipstick to find out how harmful it is. Factory farms populated with a breed of super animals that have become nothing more than ultra-efficient meat, milk and egg machines on legs for a nation that already has more food than it can eat. No one likes to dwell on these images because they involve animal suffering and the knowledge that we benefit directly from their suffering. But which experiments are you prepared to eliminate? Which benefits are you prepared to give up?

DO WE HAVE TO USE ANIMALS IN RESEARCH?

> *'The British Medical Association believes that animal experimentation is necessary at present to develop a better understanding of diseases and how to treat them, but believes that, when possible, alternative methods should be used.'*
> **British Medical Association**

Animal experimentation is only one of many research tools and a researcher frequently combines it with other, non-animal methods of research. When a researcher sets out to test a new idea about, say, a new treatment for cancer, he or she will first review other researchers' experiments and results to avoid duplicating their work. This will have an impact on the number of animals used each year. Next the researcher has to design the experiment and decide what types of research methods are likely to produce the information needed. He or she will consider whether the non-animal methods that follow will do the job.

1 Use people

➤You probably aren't surprised to learn that the most reliable results come from studying human beings. Animals inhaled tobacco smoke for many years in laboratories as researchers tried to discover whether there was a link between smoking and lung cancer. But no matter how long they puffed, animals failed to develop lung cancer – a result that gladdened the hearts of tobacco company executives but which probably sentenced thousands more people to death from smoking-related lung cancer because governments delayed warning people of the dangers of smoking. Proof of the link finally came from a large study of doctors – some smokers, some non-smokers.

Another example of the good results that can follow this type of research (known as epidemiology) occurred in the 1960s. At that time, survival rate for childhood leukaemia was poor. A careful study of the treatments and responses of many patients gradually revealed that a particular combination of drugs plus radiotherapy gave the best results. When this combination treatment became standard, survival rates quickly rose to 70 per cent. It is hoped that a similar approach might uncover the best form of treatment for breast cancer. This kind of research was one of the tools used to pinpoint the role that a high-fat diet, smoking, drinking and lack of exercise play in the development of heart disease. Using human volunteers has the added advantage that they can test new drugs and tell researchers how they feel afterwards.

> 'There are some side-effects which will never show up in animal tests because animals cannot tell researchers how they are feeling. So side effects such as nausea, headaches, depression and dizziness will never be discovered until they are experienced by people.'
> The Humane Research Trust

2 Use parts of people

►The thought of using little pieces from people's bodies to experiment on might make you feel a bit squeamish, but it works. Cells are the basic units that make up all living things, and your body is made up of billions of them.

Tissues such as your muscle or nerves are made up of groups of cells that all do the same thing. Organs such as your liver or lungs are, in turn, made up of different types of tissues. Researchers can either work with a single layer of cells grown in a plastic dish or test-tube, or with small pieces of tissue or even slices of organ.

Where do they get their supply of human tissue? From many sources including patients, volunteers, dead bodies that have been donated to science or been autopsied, blood, foetuses, afterbirth material from maternity wards, tissues and body parts removed during surgery and so on. Researchers can already do many things with tissue cultures that were once done with animals and will soon be able to do many more. These include:

- *Developing vaccines.* Human cells are now used to prepare a rabies vaccine that is ten times more powerful and virtually free of the side-effects that were common when it used to be prepared in duck embryos.
- *Developing antibodies.* Antibodies occur naturally in the body and their job is to recognize and attack foreign invaders. If researchers need a supply of antibodies they have to grow them in large tumours inside mice. Soon they'll be able to produce antibodies from human tissue, which means they'll be better suited than mice antibodies for the treatment of people.
- *Making diagnoses.* The only way to diagnose TB in the past was to inject infected tissue into guinea pigs then kill them several weeks later to see if they had developed the disease. The use of a tissue culture produces faster results and spares the lives of thousands of guinea pigs each year. Likewise, the use of tissue culture has speeded up the diagnosis time for rabies from 35 to four days and spares the lives of thousands of mice.

- *Testing for toxicity.* Human cell-based tests are now being used to replace Draize eye and skin irritancy tests (growing human skin is one option) and cell tests can also detect substances likely to cause cancer.
- *Developing drugs.* It's now possible to use cell cultures to test chemicals and to study their effects on tissues throughout the development of the drug.

The advantage of using tissue cultures is that researchers can study specific tissues and need only small doses of chemicals. The disadvantage is that the researcher cannot achieve full information about how the whole body reacts, only selected parts of it.

> *The RSPCA is opposed to all experiments that cause pain, suffering or distress to animals. Its ultimate goal is to see animal experiments replaced by humane alternatives, with the reduction of animal use and animal suffering as its immediate objectives.*

'EYTEX and SKINTEX are chemical tests, carried out in a test-tube, which can be used to replace the Draize eye and skin irritancy tests for many chemicals... Unfortunately, however, industry still invests far too little in the development of humane alternative tests and even where such techniques are available they are often not used because governments continue to demand that animal tests be carried out.'
British Union for the Abolition of Vivisection

3 Use micro-organisms

▶Micro-organisms such as yeast and bacteria are alive yet they have no awareness, which means they feel no pain. This makes them ideal candidates for helping us out by doing such things as:

• *Testing skin irritation.* Certain drugs and perfumes contain chemicals that can cause irritation on human skin when it's exposed to sunlight. Yeast grown in plastic dishes and exposed to these same chemicals is affected in the same way by light. Two types of yeast can now prevent the suffering of thousands of rabbits, rats, hairless mice, guinea pigs and pigs.

• *Making useful products.* By inserting genes from other cells into bacteria, researchers can make them produce insulin identical to that made by humans. They can also be made to produce vaccines, enzymes, growth hormones and monoclonal antibodies (proteins that identify, measure and purify substances). Until bacteria could be used this way, thousands of rats, mice and rabbits were subjected to painful processes to produce monoclonal antibodies.

• *Testing eye irritancy.* Protozoa are single-celled organisms found in ponds. They can be easily recognized under a microscope because they always use the same pattern of movements when they swim. When a harmful substance is added to the water, however, this pattern changes. Researchers use this behaviour change to predict the harmfulness of test substances. It is a simple, inexpensive alternative to the Draize eye irritancy test using rabbits.

• *Testing for toxicity.* Marine bacteria that glow in the dark when healthy, dim considerably when damaged by harmful chemicals. Sensitive laboratory equipment can measure the change in the light they emit and use the information to predict the harmfulness of test chemicals. The Microtox toxicity test, as it's known, has been used successfully to test water samples, household products, industrial waste and chemicals and has saved the lives of thousands of mice, rabbits and fish.

• *Testing for birth defects.* Hydra is a very simple multicelled organism that lives in water. It's remarkable in that it can be broken up into individual cells and within hours it will have pulled itself back together again as if nothing had happened. A simple test for detecting chemicals likely to cause birth defects involves breaking a hydra into pieces then exposing it to a chemical. If the chemical prevents the Hydra from reforming itself, it's also likely to interfere with the normal development of an embryo. (hydra was able to recognize the notorious drug Thalidomide, which caused so many birth defects, as harmful.) The use of hydra can save large numbers of rats, mice, rabbits and monkeys from inhumane treatment, as well as saving money and time.

• *Testing for cancer-causing substances.* Carcinogens are chemicals that cause cancers. Two types of bacteria can detect certain types of carcinogens, which should take some of the pressure off rats and mice that are fed carcinogenic substances every day of their lives.

'Recent research shows that many animal experiments use more animals than are scientifically necessary because they are poorly designed, which can also lead to misinterpretation of results.'
Bob Combes, Scientific Director, FRAME

4 Use computers

►It's now possible to carry out research on a computer by creating models of parts of the human body. For instance, one group of researchers created a computer simulation of how the brain works. When they simulate injury to the brain, the computer mimics the symptoms of the injured person. Another group of researchers took ten years to create a model of 10,000 brain cells (they started out with a network of about 100 cells) that has given them clues about how brain disorders like epilepsy develop. Imagine their surprise when one day, their computer model began to act like a real brain by spontaneously producing electrical signals similar to those that animals' brains make when they're resting! If you have access to the Internet, you can visit Cybermouse. It's an on-line, virtual lab animal that can be used by scientists to explore the immune system.

Scientists claim they can run experiments on Cybermouse that would take too much time or be too difficult to do with live animals. Cybermouse is being used to predict how the Aids virus spreads through the human immune system. Researchers can also use sophisticated computer programs to assess the safety of new drugs or household, agricultural and industrial chemicals. COMPACT, a computer program that creates a 3-D image of the molecular structure of substances so that it can recognize any that have harmful shapes, has a higher accuracy rate than most of the accepted animal safety tests. Computer simulations might take the place of LD50 and Draize eye irritancy tests, and are already saving the lives of thousands of small mammals and amphibians that would have been dissected by college and university students.

Did you know?

In November 1996, The Body Shop presented a four-million-signature petition to the European Commission calling for it to implement the proposed ban on the sale of animal-tested cosmetics within the European Union. Instead of being enforced, the ban was postponed until at least 1 January 2000 on the grounds that alternative test methods have not been scientifically accepted according to the standards of the Organization for Economic Cooperation and Development (OECD). This organization includes Japan and the US, two countries whose cosmetic industries use animal testing extensively.

5 Use other technology

➤Have you seen films of crash test dummies in operation on TV? Their advanced technology allows them to react to crash situations as if they were human. Crashing a dummy into a brick wall at 60 km/h (40 mph) is certainly preferable to doing the same to a baboon or rhesus monkey. (In one experiment, four rhesus monkeys were each crashed eight times. The unsurprising conclusion reached was that the more forceful the crash, the more damage was done to the animals' nervous systems!) Doctors can also learn how to give anaesthetics safely by practising on a dummy that breathes and reacts just like a human.

If researchers have all of these alternative methods of research at their disposal, why do they still use animals? If the safety of a product is in question, UK, European and international laws have a big say in how safety tests are carried out. Traditionally, the scientific basis for safety testing involves animal tests and it takes time to change from traditional to new ways of doing things. First, governments have to be convinced that they have a moral responsibility to consider using alternatives to animals. Then they have to be convinced that the alternatives can be scientifically proven to be reliable. And there's still the matter of needing to know how new drugs affect the whole body, not just little bits and pieces of it. Until that problem is solved and government regulations are changed, scientists will have to continue using animals as the safety buffer between test-tube testing and human testing. Back in 1958 two researchers proposed a set of guiding principles for anyone working with laboratory animals so that their welfare could be improved quickly regardless of how long it took for big changes to happen. They're known as the three R's of humane animal research and all reputable researchers follow them:

1 Reduce the number of animals used in experiments.
2 Refine experiments to keep suffering to a minimum.
3 Replace animals with new techniques wherever possible.

WHAT CAN YOU DO?

Ask the RSPCA (address on page 221) for a copy of their cruelty-free product guide, *Think before you shop*, and their leaflet *Putting the Message Across,* and follow their suggestions. Then take a good look around your home, because your actions there can reduce the demand for laboratory animals in the future. Start in the kitchen and work your way through the house, checking off any animal-tested products you find as well as any actions you're prepared to take.

Animals under the kitchen sink

☐ Kitchen cleansers
☐ Washing powders or liquids
☐ Disinfectants
☐ Anti-pest products
☐ Polishes
☐ Any products marked 'new' and/or 'improved'

➤ Take a quick look at their labels and note how many chemicals they contain. Most of these will have been tested on animals in the past. Anything with a 'new' or 'improved' tag on it will probably have been tested recently on animals.

What I'm prepared to do

☐ Persuade my family to stop buying products marked 'new and improved'.
☐ If I do the shopping, I won't buy 'new and improved' products.
☐ Find out how to clean a house using traditional cleansers (bleach, household ammonia, vinegar,

bicarbonate and washing soda).

☐ Offer to help clean the house using traditional cleansers (tip: vinegar and newspaper make windows sparkle).

Animals in the kitchen cupboards

☐ Any processed foods

►Check the labels on tins and packaging and you'll discover that most processed foods are full of additives such as preservatives, artificial food colours, flavourings and all kinds of 'improvers'. Each one of these will probably have been tested on animals.

What I'm prepared to do

☐ Try to wean myself off processed 'convenience' foods.

☐ Suggest that we try to buy less processed and more natural foods.

☐ Offer to help prepare natural foods for cooking.

☐ Suggest we buy some of our food from a health food shop and look for labels that say 'no artificial additives'.

Animals in the fridge

☐ Non-organic fruits and vegetables

►Most fruits and vegetables you buy at supermarkets are grown using fertilizers and large doses of weed-killers, pesticides and fungicides. Most of them are poisonous and will probably have been force-fed to animals in LD50 tests. (For a list of supermarkets that sell organic produce, see page 107.)

What I'm prepared to do

☐ Suggest that we look for a store that sells organic fruits and vegetables.
☐ Offer to help look after the vegetable garden.

Animals in the bathroom

☐ Shampoo and conditioner
☐ Soap
☐ Toothpaste and mouthwash
☐ Face creams and lotions
☐ Shaving soaps and aftershave lotions
☐ Deodorants
☐ Bathroom cleansers
☐ Hair products
☐ Cosmetics
☐ Medicines (prescription and across-the-counter)

➤Check to see if the toiletries and cosmetics in your bathroom have been tested on animals. (See 'How to recognize a cruelty-free product' below.) Remember, even if a company claims that its product hasn't been tested on animals, chances are its ingredients have been in the past. All medicines in your bathroom cupboard will have been developed and tested using laboratory animals.

What I'm prepared to do

☐ Try to buy toiletries and cosmetics from companies (e.g. Beauty Without Cruelty and Body Shop) that do not use any ingredients that might have been tested on animals after a fixed date, e.g. 1976.
☐ Avoid buying any product marked 'new' and/or 'improved'.

☐ Ask myself whether I really need to buy so many personal hygiene or cosmetic products.

☐ Try to stay healthy so I don't need to take medicine (eat a sensible diet, don't smoke, stay away from alcohol and get plenty of exercise and sleep).

☐ If I get sick, ask my doctor if it's possible to try an alternative treatment besides drugs.

Animals in the bedroom

☐ Cotton clothes and bedding not organically produced
☐ Wool jumpers and blankets
☐ Leather clothes and shoes
☐ Sheepskin coat
☐ Clothes made out of synthetic materials

➤The traditional way of producing cotton requires massive amounts of pesticides as well as many chemicals used to bleach, dye and process the fabric. (All these chemicals have to be tested on animals.) The vaccines and drugs used to keep wool-bearing sheep disease-free all have to be tested. Leather and sheepskins have to be treated with preservatives and other chemicals, and they have to be tested. And many of the raw materials and chemicals used in the production of synthetic fabrics will have been safety tested too.

What I'm prepared to do

☐ Try to buy organically produced cotton clothes, bedding and towels.

☐ Buy the best quality, classically-styled clothes that you can afford so that they last.

☐ Try not to buy clothes that go quickly out of fashion.

☐ Recycle your clothes.

☐ Ask yourself whether you really need to buy so many clothes.

❏ How to recognize a cruelty-free product

The RSPCA has analysed labels on hundreds of products and they conclude that labelling doesn't always mean what you think it means. So beware when you see apparently animal-friendly statements like these:

'Against animal testing' (Anyone can say this, it doesn't mean they do anything about it.)

'Product not tested on animals' It's individual ingredients that are usually tested, not necessarily the product they all combine to make.)

'Our company does not initiate tests' (Again, this could be true, but it doesn't say that the company's suppliers, or even another company doesn't test on their behalf.)

'Product contains 'natural' ingredients' (Even natural products have to be tested if their safety is questioned.)

So how can you tell cruelty-free products from the rest? Look for a claim on the label that says the company doesn't use any ingredients which were tested on animals after a specified date. Look for something as specific as a fixed cut-off date, as in, 'will not use any ingredients tested on animals by our company or on our behalf after January, 1976'. If in doubt, write to the managing director of the company and ask for information on his or her company's policy on testing ingredients or products on animals. Be sure to ask if the company has a fixed cut-off date.

> *'The RSPCA believes the fixed cut-off date is the best and only truly cruelty-free policy because it immediately avoids the use of new ingredients and, therefore, animal tests.'*
> *Think before you shop...Cruelty-free product guide, RSPCA 1995*

You needn't confine your activities on behalf of animals to your home. If, for instance, you object to dissecting animals at school, you needn't do so. Although teachers are free to include dissection in the curriculum if they wish, the law does not require any pupils under the age of 16 to dissect animals, nor is it compulsory at A-levels. There are plenty of other ways to find out how animal bodies work and your teacher will probably have access to them. You can even dissect a cyberfrog on the Internet. The site address is *http://www.teach.virginia.edu/go/frog*

What's your opinion?
It's time to go back to see what you thought about the statements at the beginning of this section and find out if you've changed your mind about any of them. Science plays an important, often hidden, role in all our lives. But, important as science is, it's still only one aspect of our lives. Just because things are done in the name of science 'for our own good' doesn't mean that we shouldn't question them.

Many people found it relatively simple to make the decision that animals shouldn't suffer for something as frivolous as cosmetics or bubble bath and wholeheartedly supported the first cosmetic companies to turn their backs on animal testing. But what do you say 'no' to next? Many might also be willing to give up safety testing of household products on animals but might want to continue using them in medical research because they believe the benefits to us far outweigh the costs to the animals.

Of course, not everyone is overjoyed at the benefits the advances of medical science have reaped and might claim that we expect far too much from it. We're living longer yes. But what's the point of living longer if you can't enjoy life? The longer we live the more likely it is that we'll succumb to one of the terrible diseases of old age, like Alzheimer's, for which modern medicine has no answer. Ask someone in their 80s or 90s, who is terminally ill after a long illness and is being kept alive by medicines and machines, what he or she thinks of the advances of modern medicine. As promised at the beginning of this book, there is nothing black or white about the issues surrounding animal research, and there are no easy answers.

Here's one final thought. Every year, people in Britain consume more than 750 million animals as meat — about 280 times the number of animals used in research?

Stop press!

In November 1997 all cosmetic companies in Britain that had not already done so agreed to an immediate voluntary ban on the use of animals to test cosmetic products. Testing of cosmetic ingredients, however, will continue. Lord Williams, Home Office minister, said he would now consider a ban on the safety testing of cosmetic ingredients to eliminate animal research altogether from the production of cosmetics.

QUIZ

A brain scrambler

When you've found all the words in the list (and remember they can go up, down, forwards, backwards and diagonally) circle the remaining letters and put them in the blanks below to discover an important question about animals.

___ _____ __ ___, ___ ____
_____? ___ ____ ____? ___ ___
____ _____?

Jeremy Bentham, philosopher (1748-1832)

AID (AS IN ANIMAL AID)
ALTERNATIVE
AMR (ANIMALS IN
MEDICINES RESEARCH)
ANAESTHETICS
ANIMAL RESEARCH
ANTIBODIES
BACTERIA
BIOLOGY
BUAV (BRITISH UNION
FOR THE ABOLITION OF
VIVISECTION)
CAGES
CANCER
CATS
CELLS
COMPUTER
COSMETICS
CTPA (COSMETICS
TOILETRY AND PERFUMERY

ASSOCIATION)
DNA
DRAIZE
DRUG
EPIDEMIOLOGY
EYES
FRAME (FUND FOR THE
REPLACEMENT OF
ANIMALS IN MEDICAL
EXPERIMENTS)
GENE
HIV
IMMUNITY
MEDICINE
MICE
MONKEY
PAIN
PAINKILLER
POISON
POLIO

Y	T	I	N	U	M	M	I	T	E	H	E	S	I	M	R	M	A
F	R	A	M	E	E	Q	U	U	E	P	R	H	C	G	S	N	L
T	D	E	I	E	Y	E	S	T	I	B	B	A	R	O	I	C	T
N	R	R	L	I	D	S	S	D	S	E	G	A	C	M	E	G	E
N	A	E	U	L	I	I	E	D	N	A	E	C	A	L	P	E	R
S	I	T	F	T	I	M	C	O	T	B	C	L	L	A	N	N	N
T	Z	U	A	T	I	K	H	I	U	E	R	S	Y	R	E	E	A
A	E	P	W	O	A	S	N	A	N	E	C	T	P	A	O	N	T
C	C	M	L	A	V	I	V	I	S	E	C	T	I	O	N	N	I
Y	G	O	L	O	I	B	T	E	A	S	E	N	I	C	C	A	V
R	G	C	H	E	T	R	A	N	S	P	L	A	N	T	S	I	E
Y	E	A	S	T	Y	R	C	T	A	O	H	D	S	T	A	R	L
T	K	D	B	U	C	A	P	E	N	I	F	E	R	T	C	E	O
E	M	A	U	H	N	A	I	D	V	S	N	T	D	U	H	T	I
F	I	E	S	C	I	T	E	M	S	O	C	Y	S	S	G	C	L
A	C	U	E	N	E	R	E	E	T	N	U	L	O	V	F	A	O
S	E	R	A	N	T	I	B	O	D	I	E	S	F	E	R	B	P
Y	E	K	N	O	M	S	C	I	T	E	H	T	S	E	A	N	A

RABBITS
RATS
RDS (RESEARCH DEFENCE SOCIETY)
REDUCE
REFINE
REPLACE
RHCG (RESEARCH FOR HEALTH CHARITIES GROUP)
SAFETY
SIMR (SERIOUSLY ILL FOR MEDICAL RESEARCH)
TISSUE
TRANSPLANTS
UFAW (THE UNIVERSITIES FEDERATION FOR ANIMAL WELFARE)
VACCINES
VIVISECTION
VOLUNTEER
YEAST

(Answer page 224)

Section Four

ANIMAL RIGHTS

> *'Animals of the world exist for their own reason. They were not made for humans any more than black people were made for whites or women for men.'*
> **Alice Walker, writer**

People everywhere, regardless of whether their skin is white, yellow or brown, whether they're male or female, British or Zimbabwean, or whether they believe in God, Buddha or Mother Nature, suffer in the same way and for similar reasons. Only relatively recently have we come to accept that all people, whatever their colour, race, sex or beliefs, should enjoy equal rights because they care equally about what happens to them.

If you had to choose between going hungry and eating, you'd choose to eat. Animals would do the same because they too would choose not to suffer. Does this mean that, like us, they care about what happens to them? If so, shouldn't we treat them with the kind of consideration we reserve for ourselves? You can see where this kind of thinking is leading. If animals deserve to be treated considerately because, like us, they're aware enough to care about what happens to them, don't we have the responsibility to make sure they don't suffer?

> *'It is meaningless to talk of animal rights because rights are one side of a moral contract, the other being responsibilities. If animals have rights, then gazelles have a grievance against lions.'*
> **Bryan Appleyard, journalist**

There has been a great deal of talk in recent years about animal rights and a number of straight-thinking people have put forward their ideas. Some claim that animals can have neither rights nor duties because they cannot grasp any moral idea, such as 'Thou shalt not kill'. (We're back to the bear who killed the salmon in Section Two and could not be held responsible for its actions because it's not a moral being.) They argue that you cannot have rights without responsibilities. How does that work? Let's say you buy a stereo. You have the right to play it whenever you wish. So let's say you wish to play it at four o'clock in the morning. Because your family and neighbours also have rights, in this case backed up by the Environmental Protection Act that frowns upon disturbance of the peace at four o'clock in the morning, you have the responsibility to respect their rights and play your stereo in a way that doesn't disturb them. (Try the headphones.) If you insist on thinking only about your own rights and ignore the rights of others, eventually, in this instance, the law will help you remember them. So, in this argument, rights and responsibilities go hand in hand and you can't have one without the other. Because animals are not moral beings and cannot be held responsible for their actions, this argument concludes that they cannot have rights.

We are trying very hard to stamp out all kinds of prejudices that harm other people and deny them equal rights. Racism, sexism and a whole host of other 'isms' are being dragged out of the dark cupboard we've stuffed them into for centuries and are being given a thorough shake out and airing. So far, we don't seem to have given much airing to speciesism – a lack of concern for a member of another species simply because it doesn't belong to our own species.

What happens, asks another group of straight thinkers, when you apply the same argument to humans who cannot yet be classed as moral beings – babies? Human babies aren't born with language and moral concepts, so before they achieve them they, like animals, cannot be held responsible for their actions. Yet they have the right to be cared for properly and not to be harmed. That right is conferred on them by adults who take it upon themselves to speak up for babies when they see grounds for complaint. If human babies can be granted rights on the basis of there being grounds for complaint about their treatment, why can't animals? If neither human babies nor animals are moral beings, and we can speak up for babies, why can't we also speak up for animals?

> *'The real issue is this. Are there certain things which it is wrong to do to animals for essentially the same reasons as it is wrong to do them to humans? If there are, and if we talk of the rights of humans in this connection, it is important to talk of the rights of animals in this connection too.'*
> **Timothy L.S. Sprigge, St. Andrew Animal Fund**

If you live in the western world, you'll have many different kinds of rights. The right to go about your business without interference (providing it's on the right side of the law). The right to free speech. The right to have an education. The right not to be tortured or killed for your political beliefs. The list goes on. All these rights of yours are respected only if people live up to their responsibilities and either don't interfere with you or help you when you need it. Some rights are guaranteed by law (such as not having to put up with loud music every morning at four o'clock from the house next door), others are moral. If you have a moral right to avoid suffering, for instance, because you care about what happens to you, there are grounds for complaint on your behalf against anyone who interferes with your efforts to gain relief from suffering or fails in their duty to help you gain it.

Accepting that animals have the same moral right to avoid suffering that we have hinges on whether they care about what happens to them, and also on whether they suffer from the way we treat them. The assumption throughout this book has been that they *do* care and they *do* suffer. (And if we've ever been uncertain, we've probably been willing to give them the benefit of the doubt.) But assumptions are one thing, certainty is another. You can see how our attitudes would have to change towards animals if we ever became certain that they *do* think, remember, look forward to things happening, feel happy, sad or afraid.

Animals have moral rights because:
- They are thinking, feeling beings, aware of their own suffering.
- They care what happens to them just as we care what happens to us.

Animals have no moral rights because:
- No one knows for certain how aware they are.
- No one knows for certain whether they suffer like we do.

What's your opinion?
Are you ready to dig down deep and see what you come up with in response to these statements?

1 Because animals can't talk, they can't think or be aware of themselves.
Agree ☐   Disagree ☐   Unsure ☐

2 Animals don't feel pain like we do.
Agree ☐   Disagree ☐   Unsure ☐

3 Animals have the moral right to avoid suffering.
Agree ☐   Disagree ☐   Unsure ☐

4 The Five Freedoms needn't apply to pets.
Agree ☐   Disagree ☐   Unsure ☐

5 It is morally wrong for us to use animals for our gain.
Agree ☐   Disagree ☐   Unsure ☐

DO ANIMALS THINK?

> *'If we decide that other animals are not conscious, then possibly we can get on with our meals and eradicate pests and do all sorts of things to them without being disturbed by the moral issues that might trouble us if we thought they were.'*
> **Marion Stamp Dawkins, biologist**

Consciousness is one of the greatest mysteries still to be solved. No one quite knows what it is and whether it has evolved as a survival tool in many other animals besides humans. We assume we know what other people think and feel because we can identify with what they do, and we can read the expressions on their faces and their unspoken body language. Also they can tell us. But we don't know for sure because we can't get inside their heads to think their thoughts or feel their emotions. We can only think and feel our own.

How much more difficult it is, then, to figure out what animals are thinking or feeling when they can't even tell us. In recent years, scientists have been able to design experiments that allow them to work out what goes on inside animals' heads by the things they do and the choices they make. But the idea that animals really could be aware met with a lot of resistance and was slow to take hold. It wasn't always so.

Back in 1871 when Charles Darwin wrote *The Descent of Man*, it was fashionable to accept that animals had the same senses, intuitions, emotions, curiosity and other mental states as humans, only less so. (The thinking went something like this: animals couldn't possibly be as advanced as humans because we were on the top rung of the evolution ladder, but they could share some of our wonderful faculties even if they were several rungs below us.)

> **Believe it or not!**
> *Kanzi, a bonobo or pygmy chimp, learned to understand spoken English so well that researchers eventually had to spell out some words, just as parents do when they don't want young children to understand what they are saying.*

This was still common belief in the early 1900s when a retired German mathematics professor called Herr von Osten discovered that his horse, Hans, seemed to be particularly bright. The professor promptly gave Hans lessons in music, spelling and counting, threw in some simple arithmetic for good measure, upgraded his horse's name to Clever Hans and started making lots of money out of public performances. Whenever people gave Clever Hans sums to do, he would tap his foot the correct number of times in answer. Hans made lots of friends for Herr von Osten and influenced people – except for one Doubting Thomas by the name of Oskar Pfungst (with an almost silent P).

After investigating Hans' gifts in depth, Pfungst concluded that not only did the horse not know the answers to the problems posed to him, but also he couldn't even understand the questions. By ruling out one possibility after another, Pfungst determined that Hans was simply picking up cues from whoever asked him the questions. If, for instance, Hans was asked to provide the answer to 5 + 7, he'd start tapping his hoof. The questioner, who knew the correct answer, would relax as soon as the horse tapped his hoof for the twelfth time. Hans, being skilled at reading subtle body language in other horses, would notice the slight lift of a head, or the release of shoulder tension, and immediately stop tapping.

> **What the experience with Clever Hans revealed, of course, is that horses, and many other animals, don't need to speak a human language to understand us. They read subtle body language like a book.**

The debunking of the Clever Hans myth was one of the events that put the idea of animal awareness back into the closet and slammed the door on it for the next 70 years. During that time, scientists stuck to observing animal behaviours they could see and measure, and ridiculed any scientist who suggested there might be more going on inside animals' heads than met the eye. Then, in 1976, Donald Griffin prised open the closet door with his book *The Question of Animal Awareness*. In it, he argued that intelligence and self-awareness are such useful things to have for survival that they are exactly the kinds of characteristics natural selection would favour – not just in humans, but in other animals too. He even went so far as to claim that bees could think and birds knew what they were doing when they deceived their enemies or other birds. The book caused an uproar but, because Griffin was such a respected scientist, it also signalled the beginning of a major shift in the way scientists thought about animal minds, which eventually resulted in new research into the way animals think.

What do you think?

Every animal on Earth, human and non-human, has the survival instinct. One of the survival tools we developed was consciousness (whatever it is!). In fact, we developed it so well we took over and became Boss Species of planet Earth. Evolution has a habit of repeating its successes. So what's to prevent other animals from also developing consciousness for the same reason and in similar ways?

What do you do when you think? You carry on a mental conversation with yourself. If you're solving a problem, it might go something like, 'Hmm. How do I make sure Jim and I end up with equal size pieces of chocolate cake when he's not going to let me cut it? I know, I'll suggest that he cut the cake and I choose which of the two pieces he gets.' What are some of the other things you do? You remember people, places, smells, images, tastes, feelings from the past and you anticipate things happening in the future. You might even become anxious or afraid about some upcoming event. You're aware of yourself thinking and doing things and know you're a separate being that can be threatened by things going on outside of you. You have likes and dislikes, and often tell others what you want.

You'll notice that this list, which isn't complete by any means, begins and ends with language, which has become crucial to the way we think. Try thinking without words and see where you get. Does this mean animals that have no spoken language cannot think? Not necessarily. Humans haven't always had a spoken language. Our brains gradually developed the capacity for language as we evolved as social beings. If you want to see a human who can think without language, watch how a baby learns without it. A baby can think long before it learns to speak. If it couldn't, it would stand no chance of learning language in the first place. Researchers have even discovered that very young babies possess basic number skill – for instance, they know when something is missing. But then, so do monkeys, and even some birds know how to count.

❏ Bird brains

A researcher called Koehler demonstrated that a raven and a grey parrot could learn to count up to six. Out of sight of the birds, he hid food in one of five small test boxes. Each box had a different number of dots on its lid, ranging from two to six. The birds could discover which box contained the food by looking at a separate sample box, which might have anything from two to six spots on its lid. Then they had to find the test box that had the same number of spots. Neither bird had trouble grasping the concept of number, and they did it without language.

Did you know?

Charles, a gorilla at the Metropolitan Toronto Zoo, surprised the researcher who was working with him by showing that he could count up to four with no training at all. The researcher wanted to know how well Charles could remember where to find food, so every day she hid eight containers in his enclosure but only ever put food in four of them. It didn't take Charles long to catch on. He'd open containers until he found food in four of them, then wouldn't bother with the rest.

Deciding that language isn't necessary for thinking takes us a step closer to accepting animals as thinking beings. But how can you check to see if animals have self-awareness? A researcher called Gallup decided that if he could prove that chimpanzees realized they were seeing themselves when they looked in a mirror, this would be a good test of self-awareness. (Not all scientists agree with him.) He used chimpanzees who were already familiar with mirrors and gave them a mild anaesthetic so that he could dab red dye on their eyebrows and ears without them knowing anything about it. When the chimps woke up, and saw their reflections in the mirror, to Gallup's delight, they immediately picked at the red spots on their faces. Why else would the chimps do this, Gallup argued, if they didn't realize that it was their own face they were seeing in the mirror?

If chimps are aware that they're looking at themselves in a mirror, what about some of their close relatives? Orangutans aced the same mirror test but, alas, gorillas drew a blank. Gallup could only conclude that gorillas are not truly conscious, as you, chimps and orangutans are, because they're not aware that they're aware. (Tricky, isn't it?) In other words, they don't look in the mirror and think to themselves (in gorilla thought), 'I'm sitting here looking at myself in a mirror, so that face looking back at me isn't me but a reflection of me. Hang on a minute, who's been putting red dots on my face while I've been taking 40 winks?' It's difficult to believe that two of our closest primate relatives have self-awareness while the third doesn't. One philosopher suggested that perhaps gorillas recognize themselves in mirrors but don't show it. Tongue in cheek, he also suggested that gorillas might have evolved close to crocodile-infested waters, which would have really cramped the style of any gorilla who was foolish enough to spend time admiring its own reflection!

Did you know?

A research team trained rats to press one of four levers to show what they were doing when a buzzer sounded. If the rats were washing their faces when the buzzer rang, they'd press the face-washing lever, if they were walking about they'd press the walking-about lever and so on. Each time they pressed the lever that corresponded to what they were doing, the rats received a food reward. The conclusion? Either rats are aware of their own actions or they're very good at playing the games we create for them.

If you applied common sense to the question of self-awareness, you might argue that one way to discover whether animals are aware of themselves or not is to find out if they know the difference between what happens to them and what doesn't. Apparently, they do. Even octopuses, which are as unlike humans as you can get, know when they are being touched as opposed to when they're doing the touching. The fact that animals react to something they think is threatening could, in itself, be taken as evidence of some level of self-awareness. If they weren't conscious of themselves being threatened by something outside of themselves, why would they react at all?

You demonstrate an ability for 'equivalence thinking' in maths when you show that if A = B and B = C, then A must also = C. Don't feel too smug. A sea lion named Rio can do exactly the same!

❑ Suckered!

The octopus is one of those animals without backbones (an invertebrate) that looks as alien to us as if it came from another planet. Yet inside that odd-shaped head lurks a formidable brain which, even though it differs from a mammal's brain, allows the octopus to solve problems, learn complicated tasks and remember what it has learned for several weeks. For example, two scientists built an upside-down maze with doors. The octopus was supposed to swim through the maze, learning which doors opened in and which opened out so that it could reach the food at the centre of the maze. The octopus considered the problem, paused, then lifted the entire maze out of the way so that it could reach underneath and grab the food. When the embarrassed scientists anchored the maze down, the octopus had no choice but to quickly work out which doors to pull and which to push to get at the food.

We've looked at evidence that suggests animals can think without benefit of a complex, spoken language and seen how self-awareness might not be something that only humans possess. But do animals have concepts like we do? Do they, for example, remember things from the past, or look forward to things happening in the future? They certainly behave as if they do. One scientist reported that his dog always made a point of leaving some of his breakfast in his bowl so that he too would have something to eat when his human family ate lunch. Why would the dog do this if he had no memory of what had happened yesterday lunchtime and couldn't look forward to the same thing happening at lunchtime today? Even rats that usually are rewarded with a treat when they reach the end of a maze become very ratty if the treat isn't there, and run up and down looking for it. Is that anticipation, or what?

If an animal solves a problem that it's never come across before, it's seen as proof that it's worked things out for itself, rather than relied on instinct. In one experiment, a chimpanzee demonstrated a great knack for using abstract concepts to solve problems. The chimp was presented with the problem of an out-of-reach banana. But instead of being offered something concrete to stand on to reach the banana, it was shown two photographs – one of a hose and one of a stool – and was asked to pick the photo of the object that could solve the problem. With no hesitation, the chimp chose the photo of the stool. The experiment showed that the chimp could push ideas around in its mind just as easily as it could push objects around its cage.

❑ Water on the brain

How is a canary similar to a daffodil? If the answer 'yellow' pops into your head, it's because your brain is good at classifying things and correctly identifies two very differently-shaped objects as belonging to the same colour class. You share this ability with most mammals and birds. Pigeons, for instance, were shown hundreds of slides and had to pick out only those pictures that showed water. They did it with ease, even though the water in the pictures might be a lake, a puddle, an ocean, a glass of water, even a raindrop.

What's the alternative to animals having concepts like you? Without them, animals would have no memory of the past and would be unable to look forward to the future. They'd live completely in the now, like someone who's lost their short-term memory. Their lives would be made up of disjointed moments, brief impressions, forgotten almost as soon as they occur. This possibility is as frightening for the welfare of animals in zoos, factory farms and research laboratories as is the possibility of animals spending their time yearning for better times. Why? Because if they suffer and have no awareness of the concepts of past or future, they would have no memory of a time when they didn't suffer or anticipate a time when their suffering might end. This means they'd be stuck permanently in the present. If the present is painful, their pain would become their entire existence, relived endlessly through a series of unconnected moments. Either way, we have a responsibility to make sure animals don't suffer in our care.

> *'The assumption that animals are exactly like us except for having furry, feathery or scaly skins (is) just as ill-founded and just as misleading as the assumption that they are so unlike us that they could not possibly have any conscious experience at all.'*
> **Marion Stamp Dawkins, biologist**

DO ANIMALS SUFFER?

> *'Studies ... reveal that horses, cattle and sheep have broadly similar pain thresholds to each other and to man. When in pain, the cow may display less distress than the horse or man, but this evidence suggests that she may well experience the same intensity of pain.'*
> John Webster, Professor of Animal Husbandry

A toothache makes you suffer. It's a physical pain that can be made much worse by the anxiety you feel when you keep thinking about what the dentist might do to you. Fear, frustration, exhaustion and depression are some of the other emotional pains you can suffer. Do animals suffer both physical and emotional pain?

Physical pain

►As scientists became sceptical about animal awareness in the early 1900s and decided that animals couldn't possibly have concepts like ours, they came to believe that the physical pain animals felt was quite insignificant. Their thinking was that if animals lack concepts that allow them to remember or anticipate (and, as the toothache/dentist association demonstrates, remembering and anticipating adds to our pain) then animal pain can't be anywhere near as bad as the pain we experience. They scratched their heads in amazement when cows ate immediately after an operation, injured horses remained silent and dogs got up and moved around directly after abdominal surgery and said, 'See, if they had lasting, severe pain – like the kind we'd have in those situations – they wouldn't do these things.' If scientists and veterinarians had been able to look at the situation through the eyes of the animals, however, they might have come to a different conclusion.

Cows have been domesticated for many centuries but they've held on to all their wild instincts. In the wild, a cow that didn't graze with the rest of the herd would be picked out by predators as the most likely opportunity for dinner. Besides, the cow that misses meals is a weak cow and weak cows stand out from the rest of the herd. Another invitation for dinner!

A horse has its own way of signalling when it's in pain. Look at its eyelids. If they're tense, the horse is hurting. And dogs? Unlike upright humans whose hard-working abdominal muscles have to support the weight of their guts, four-legged dogs have a special, internal 'sling' that holds up their guts and takes the load off their muscles. The dog's anatomy means that surgery in this area shouldn't hurt as much as it does in a human. But it doesn't mean the dog is pain-free after surgery.

Another way to approach the question of whether animals feel pain is to ask whether they're physically capable of feeling pain. Your brain has a pain centre and your nervous system is very efficient at sending messages to this centre. Put your hand on a hot iron and your brain soon gets the message! In response, it releases pain-controlling substances such as serotonin, endorphin, enkephalin and substance P. If you want to dull the pain even further, you take a painkiller. If you injure yourself so badly you need surgery, an anaesthetic puts you to sleep and completely blocks out the pain.

Did you know?
Even earthworms produce endorphins to control pain.

Mammals, birds and fish all have pain control centres in their brains and all animals with backbones (vertebrates) produce pain-controlling substances similar to yours. Also, all vertebrates, and some invertebrates, react to painkillers and anaesthetics just as you do. It wouldn't make sense for them to be carrying all this pain equipment around if they didn't experience pain.

> **'Current law protects animals from acute pain associated with beating or torture but does little to protect sheep from chronic pain associated with foot-rot and nothing at all to protect broiler chickens and turkeys ... from chronic pain associated with disorders of their bones and joints.'**
> **John Webster**

If you need further convincing, ask yourself why any animal needs to feel pain. The sudden pain from a hot iron tells you to take your hand away quickly before it's badly injured. The pain of a sprained ankle forces you to rest it – exactly what it needs to heal. The very small percentage of humans who cannot feel any pain at all have to be permanently on guard against the very real possibility of seriously injuring themselves. Something as minor as a blister on the heel can become badly infected and cause dangerous blood poisoning if it's ignored, which is easy to do when it doesn't hurt. So although pain is an unpleasant experience, it's an essential one for survival.

As you discovered earlier, evolution has a habit of repeating its successful body plans. The human pain mechanism, which is what scientists call it, does its job very well, so why shouldn't it be repeated in other animals?

Physical pain causes suffering. Evidence suggests that

mammals, birds and fish are capable of feeling physical pain. Therefore it's reasonable to assume that these same animals suffer when they're in pain. But what about emotional and mental pain? Do many animals suffer from being locked up and denied the opportunity to behave normally?

> **Did you know?**
> Broiler chickens have a life expectancy of eight weeks, veal calves 12 weeks and intensively-raised pigs between 15 and 30 weeks. If they lived much longer, signs of bad health – both physical and mental – would probably start to show.

Mental and emotional pain

►Poor physical health is relatively easy to spot, but it's more difficult to know what's going on inside an animal's head. Does the polar bear pace up and down his zoo enclosure because he likes the exercise? Because he's bored? Or because he's suffering the frustration of not being able to control any aspect of his life? Marian Stamp Dawkins, the scientist who first used experiments to find out what animals really care about, suggests several questions we can ask to find out whether an animal is suffering.

> *'Communicating with animals is rather like communicating with foreigners. We must not assume that because we fail to understand them it is they who are thick.'*
> **John Webster**

QUESTION 1. DOES AN ANIMAL SUFFER BECAUSE IT CAN'T BEHAVE NATURALLY?

You've already seen in the section on factory farms how a battery hen lives compared with its wild jungle fowl ancestor. But do battery hens suffer because they can't act like jungle fowl? This a difficult question to answer because domesticated hens and jungle fowl are now quite different from each other, just as most other domesticated breeds are different from their wild ancestors. Over the years, through selective breeding, we've changed not only their body shapes and how many eggs they produce, but also how they behave. A modern jungle fowl would be shocked beyond belief by the aggression of its neighbours if it ever had the misfortune of straying into a broiler house. Besides, broiler hens and battery chickens have lived in such a different environment from jungle fowl for so long that they've probably started to adapt to it. It came as a surprise, then, to discover that some domesticated chickens released on to an uninhabited coral island off the coast of Australia soon began behaving just like wild jungle fowl.

Battery hens have shown in experiments which things are really important to them. (See **What do hens want?**, page 77.) By denying them what they want the most, we're frustrating them and making them suffer. If we're making hens suffer, we must be doing the same to animals in factory farms, research laboratories and zoos everywhere – wherever opportunities for them to behave naturally are denied.

Did you know?
In experiments to find out how important nest boxes were to hens, some birds were prepared to walk more than 1.5 kilometres around a circular corridor towards a nest box that never got any closer.

Animals behind bars might not be able to do everything they normally would in the wild, but good zoos and organic farms allow them to behave in ways that are important to them. Even research laboratories now provide animals with companions, stimulating toys and ways they can contribute to their own quality of life.

What do you think?

If a few domesticated chickens went native so quickly on a desert island, doesn't this suggests that, given half a chance, millions of battery and broiler chickens in factory farms around the world would do the same? And if they would, can we assume that they must be feeling some frustration at not being able to live like jungle fowl?

Just because an animal might be frustrated at not being able to follow through on some of its instinctive behaviours in captivity, however, doesn't mean that it misses doing everything it would have to do to survive in the wild, such as risking injury to avoid being caught by a predator. Of course, without the action, excitement and danger of avoiding predators, or finding food, or being able to woo and win a mate, life soon becomes boring.

The romantic image we have that anything an animal experiences in the wild must be good because it's free and anything it experiences in captivity must be bad because it's not free is a false one. Nothing is that black and white. Wild animals have no guarantees they won't starve to death or die from thirst. They have to compete for everything they get, and endure extreme hardships. And when death comes it's hardly ever peaceful, it's almost always painful and it can be agonizingly slow.

Did you know?

The average songbird might live for 11 years in captivity, yet survives only 1-2 years in the wild.

What do you think?

Most animals live longer in captivity than they do in the wild, but does that necessarily mean they feel better off behind bars? If animals could choose, how do we know that they wouldn't prefer a short life lived to the full in the wild to a long, safe life in captivity – even if it meant giving up the possibility of a quick, painless death for something much worse?

QUESTION 2. CAN AN ANIMAL'S BODY PROVIDE CLUES THAT IT IS SUFFERING?

When an animal suddenly comes face to face with a threatening situation, its emergency resources swing into action. Breathing and heart rate speed up to send extra oxygen around the body and the liver releases sugar for the muscles so they have the fuel they need to either fight off the danger or run away from it. When the threat is over, everything returns to normal. But if the threat doesn't go away, the animal's emergency resources remain on call. When that happens, its body begins to secrete hormones that can mobilize other forces to keep the supply of sugar flowing to the muscles. The animal is now so geared up to either fight off the enemy or put some serious mileage between them that it can hardly stand the tension. If this permanent red alert situation isn't eased, things start going wrong inside the animal's body.

These three distinct stages of changes to the animal's body are known as the General Adaptation Syndrome, or GAS for short. Scientists look for GAS changes, such as increased heart rate, enlarged adrenal glands and the release of certain hormones into the bloodstream, to tell them whether an animal is suffering. In one experiment, researchers measured hormone levels in sheep while they were being loaded into a truck, put through a sheep dip or chased by a dog. Levels of cortisone-type hormones rose in all these situations, but soared in individual sheep that were separated from the flock. To a sheep, being sent to slaughter is less of a threat than being sheared. Why? Sheep go to slaughter with the rest of the flock, they go to be sheared alone.

> **Did you know?**
> Healthy looking rats, voles and mice develop enlarged adrenal glands when they are crowded together in a small space, which suggests that overcrowding causes them to suffer despite their outward appearance.

QUESTION 3. DO ANIMALS DO ANYTHING TO SHOW THEY'RE SUFFERING?

Scientists have tried to answer this question in several ways. They've watched animals with definite GAS symptoms to see if they can connect anything they do with the changes going on inside them. They've tried scaring and frustrating animals then watched what they do. And they've watched animals who develop odd, stereotypic behaviours (such as Misha the polar bear).

It's a GAS!

►Working with animals' GAS symptoms has had mixed results, mostly because animals behave in very different ways even though the same changes might be happening inside them. The first thing most animals do when threatened, however, is turn towards whatever's doing the threatening, then blink. As heart rates increase, and adrenaline levels rise, most animals start to sweat and their hair begins to bristle. If there's no chance that they can get rid of the danger, either by fighting or running away from it, the second and third stages of the GAS are triggered. And this is where different species of animals begin to behave differently.

For instance, one GAS symptom is enlarged adrenal glands. It was discovered that chickens whose adrenal glands had enlarged the most flicked their heads the most, so increased head flicking among chickens might be taken as a visible sign of suffering. Meanwhile, rats don't flick their heads when they're confronted with bully rats that attack them and hog all the food in their cage. They very cleverly shift their daily routine so that they get up to feed after the bullies have fallen asleep.

Animals going through the early stages of GAS are often aggressive, but aggression shouldn't necessarily be taken as a sign of suffering. It's a useful survival tool in the wild and it's often used to win a mate or get a fair share of the food. The conclusions reached were that it is possible to link the changes going on inside animals' bodies with the things they do to find visible clues that they're suffering. But when a chicken flicks its head to show it's suffering, and a rat goes to sleep, you can see how impossible it is to generalize. The only way to be sure is to study every species.

❏ The final cut

Some music makes you happy, some reduces you to tears and some gives you a 'rush' and goosebumps. A researcher discovered that chickens also react emotionally to music. Every time he played Pink Floyd's 'The Final Cut' the test chickens ruffled their feathers – the bird equivalent to a goosebump-laden rush.

Not the cat's meow!

➤Scientists set up experiments in which they deliberately frustrate animals so that they can see what they do when they're frustrated. One experiment involved training cats to obtain food by pressing a switch. The cats seemed to enjoy the experience until the researcher began to frustrate them by preventing some of the switches from working. Eventually, the frustrated cats became so agitated they began pressing everything in sight, including each other.

By performing experiments like this, scientists have identified four types of behaviour that show an animal is undergoing unpleasant feelings: displacement, rebound and stereotypic behaviours and learned helplessness.

Behaviour 1: And now for something completely different...

➤You'll probably recognize displacement behaviour straight away. Two male dogs get into a scrap and one of them is forced to back down. So what does it do? It sits down and calmly begins to groom itself. Has it gone mad? No, it's simply trying to reduce its frustration by concentrating its energies on something else. People do it all the time. Next time you're witness to an argument, watch carefully to see what the loser does. Storm out, slam the door and then what? Dig the garden? Wash the dog? (Poor dog!) Play loud music? You get the idea. They're all displacement behaviours, all intended to ease frustration.

> ❏ **Arrrrggh!**
> **In its natural environment, an animal can act to control how it feels. It will, for instance, choose to do things that cause pleasure rather than suffering. In captivity, however, an animal is denied that opportunity. Visitors approaching too close to zoo animals, sows having to give birth in crates too small to turn around in, lab animals denied normal contact with others of their kind – these are all sources of suffering. But surely the greatest suffering springs from the constant frustration of not being able to do anything about it.**

Behaviour 2: On the rebound

➤If, for some reason, your dog misses its main meal of the day, you'd expect it to eat much more food at its next mealtime. In behavioural terms, when an animal is unable to do something that satisfies a behavioural need, it devotes more time to satisfying that need when the opportunity arises. Scientists look for evidence of rebound behaviour in farm animals in experiments designed to identify welfare problems.

Behaviour 3: Is there a method to this madness?

➤You've already met stereotypic behaviour in Misha the polar bear. Stereotypies either involve movement, as seen in the endless pacing of bears and big cats, the repetitive somersaults of mink, voles and chipmunks, the weaving back and forth of horses and elephants or the rocking of chimpanzees and humans. Or they involve the mouth, as seen in the bar-chewing of pigs and cows, the crib-biting and wind-sucking of horses, the tongue-rolling and sucking of veal calves and the thumb-sucking of gorillas, orangutans, chimpanzees and humans.

It's thought stereotypies are evidence of a barren environment and deprivation, but whether they're signs that the animal is trying to cope with frustration before it causes severe suffering, or whether they're signs that the animal already is suffering is not yet certain. Some scientists think that, in the right circumstances, they might simply be a sign that the animal has found a harmless, repetitive way of passing the time.

Behaviour 4: Too sad for words

►A dog that is beaten every time its owner comes home drunk will at first put on a display of submission to try to avoid the beating. As it learns that it can neither escape nor prevent the beating, its fear will grow until it leads to a state of permanent anxiety. Finally, the dog will simply give up and slip into a condition known as learned helplessness. Without hope of being able to change its situation, the dog stops responding to anything going on around it or that's done to it. In humans this is known as chronic pathological depression. Laboratory animals that can do nothing to avoid repeated procedures that cause pain develop learned helplessness. So too do pigs that cannot escape constant attacks when confined in a pen.

'Animals show unmistakable signs of suffering from pain, exhaustion, fright, frustration and so forth and the better we are acquainted with them the more readily we can detect these signs.'
Report of the Technical Committee (The Brambell Committee) to Enquire into the Welfare of Animals kept under Intensive Livestock Husbandry Systems, 1965

QUESTION 4. CAN WE FIND OUT WHAT ANIMALS WANT?

You discovered in Section Two that it's possible to have a good idea of what hens and pigs consider important to their happiness. More careful observation of animals will paint a much clearer picture of what animals want and need. It would be fine indeed if zoos, farms and research laboratories could be designed using advice from animals. Laying hens, for instance, have already disagreed with recommendations made by the Brambell Committee that the floors of their cages be made out of heavy, rectangular wire mesh. When given the choice between the new floor and the fine-gauge wire floor currently in use, the hens opted for the fine-gauge floor. So that's the way it stayed. Of course, this doesn't mean hens prefer standing on fine-gauge wire over all other surfaces. They were only given two options to choose from, so they probably saw it as the lesser of two evils.

❏ Butt out!
A researcher wanted to find out the effects of inhaling cigarette smoke over long periods so he placed mice and hamsters in individual containers and blew a steady stream of smoky

air over them. His experiment ended long before he intended it to when his research subjects told him in no uncertain terms to butt out and stop blowing smoky air over them. How? By bunging up the end of the air tube with their own faeces!

QUESTION 5. CAN WE USE OURSELVES AS MODELS FOR ANIMALS?

If you stand on a dog's paw, it jumps and yelps. Precisely what you would do in the same circumstances. So it's natural to think that the dog feels the same way you would. But unless you know for sure that a jump and yelp are outward signs that the dog is feeling pain, you can't be certain. For instance, what would you make of a cow that simply turned around and looked at you if you ran into it on your bike? Your handlebars gave it a nasty gash on its shoulder, but is it in pain? How can you tell when it's not moaning and groaning (like you probably are) or showing any outward signs of distress?

Another way of using yourself as a model is to imagine yourself in the animal's place (as you were asked to do in Section One). What must it be like to live in a battery cage, or a pig pen, or a veal crate, or a gorilla enclosure or a brightly lit laboratory? The trouble with this approach, of course, is that you can imagine yourself in a crowded pig pen, but you can't really view the experience through a pig's eyes. Things that seem ghastly to you might appear very attractive to a pig and vice versa.

Both approaches are flawed because you simply don't know enough about the animals. But scientists think that using our own experiences to help us understand animals can be worthwhile. We share a great deal in common in the way our bodies are put together and in the way we behave. Mammals, in particular, have the same emotion control centre in their brains that we do. We feel emotions and act upon them because they're useful to us. So why shouldn't animals feel emotions and act upon them because they're useful to them? Animals might not act in the same way we do, but with patience we can learn what their behaviours are telling us.

> *Humans share 98.4 per cent of their DNA with both common and pygmy chimpanzees, and approximately 97.7 per cent with gorillas. One scientist argues that humans are best classified as a third species of chimpanzee! Another points out that what's really striking about how much DNA we share with chimps is how different we turned out to be.*

When you put all the answers together to the five questions suggested by Dawkins, it's difficult not to conclude that animals are capable of suffering mental and emotional pain. One philosopher even adds another piece of evidence from what is known as the animal's *telos* – the unique set of needs and interests that characterize an animal. In other words, the dogness of the dog or the whaleness of the whale. He claims that if an animal has bones and muscles and is not allowed to use them, this alone is sufficient to cause suffering because it's thwarting the animal's most basic urges and needs. Killer whales confined in inadequate tanks, polar bears restricted to concrete pits, elephants chained up in sheds – these are all animals that would normally roam great distances throughout their lives. Like athletes in their prime, they derive pleasure from their speed, strength and stamina. It's inconceivable that they don't miss this sense of satisfaction in their own abilities. And it applies not only to large, powerful animals but to any animal that delights in its own physical prowess, whether it's a cheetah or a chipmunk.

> *'It overwhelmingly looks as though animals are conscious and suffer and, until we get evidence to the contrary, we should assume they are and do.'*
> *Bryan Appleyard, journalist*

THE FIVE FREEDOMS REVISITED

'It is clear that animals form lasting friendships, are frightened of being hunted, have a horror of dismemberment, wish they were back in the safety of their den, despair for their mates, look out for and protect their children whom they love... They feel throughout their lives, just as we do.'
Jeffrey Moussaieff Masson, Psychoanalyst and writer

The first time we visited the Five Freedoms in Section Two, we didn't question whether animals could feel physical and mental pain, or whether they suffered because they couldn't do all the things their instincts tell them they ought to be doing. Now we've asked those questions and are reasonably certain of the answers. The scientific evidence that's been gathered suggests that many animals are aware of their suffering. They feel anxious, afraid and depressed. They feel frustrated because they cannot behave normally. They think. They remember. They anticipate things happening. They're aware that things happen to them.

The Five Freedoms

1 Freedom from hunger and thirst
2 Freedom from discomfort
3 Freedom from pain, injury or disease
4 Freedom to express normal behaviour
5 Freedom from fear and distress

➤We've applied the Five Freedoms test to factory farms. Now try applying it to zoos and research laboratories and see how they rate. And then apply the same test to pets that you know. This book has concentrated on three major institutions where animals are held captive for our own benefit, but there are millions of pets in this country that also have no guarantee they'll be treated kindly.

Pets and the Five Freedoms

➤You can tell at a glance whether a dog is well cared for. His eyes sparkle, his nose is moist and his coat is thick and glossy. He's alert, friendly and obedient, full of vitality, curiosity and fun. Some of these conditions are signs of good physical health thanks to an excellent diet, plenty of fresh water and exercise, a warm, dry place to sleep at night and regular check-ups by a vet. But many of them are signs that the dog's human family is also meeting his emotional needs. He's not left alone for long periods, he has companions to play with and groom him and he socializes regularly with other dogs. Why are these things necessary for the well-being of a dog? Because a dog, like its distant relative the wolf, is a pack animal. What feels good to a dog is knowing it belongs, being sure of its place in its human 'pack' and having the social skills to get along with both humans and other dogs.

Do you think that the dog or pony that is chained up constantly with little protection from bad weather or the hot sun, with no comfortable bedding to sleep on and with no companionship is better off than a wolf or a zebra in a well run zoo? Is the bitch that lives in squalid conditions in a 'puppy mill' and is forced into one pregnancy after another to provide an endless supply of disease-prone puppies for pet shops better off than a sow or a battery hen in an intensive farming system? Or is the dog that is kicked and beaten by its owner and living in a state of constant anxiety and fear any better off than a dog in a research laboratory?

The neglected rabbit that endures life in a cage at the bottom of the garden, with little care given to its feeding, cleanliness, comfort or needs isn't suffering in the same way as the rabbits that had to endure painful 'procedures' in a research laboratory without the benefit of adequate anaesthesia, but it's suffering none the less. So too are the thousands of Christmas puppies and kittens that are abandoned each year after they've lost their appeal. What happens to them? Some starve to death or die from injury or disease. Some end up in animal shelters, where a lucky few are adopted. Some are sent to research laboratories. Large numbers are killed.

> '*Non-human animals deserve as much justice and compassion as do humans.*'
> **Andrew Tyler, Director, Animal Aid, August 1997**

But people don't have to be deliberately cruel to affect the happiness of their pets, merely careless. When a puppy or kitten first comes into a home, everyone wants to fuss over it, play with it, groom it and do all the things that form close bonds between owners and their pets. There's usually no shortage of volunteers to take frisky puppies for walks or for training sessions. But frisky puppies turn into mature dogs, which all too often lose their appeal, especially if they're badly trained. Suddenly, everyone's too busy to take the dog for a decent walk every day so that it can socialize with other dogs and find out, from smells, what's going on in the neighbourhood. No one can spare the time to play with the dog or groom it regularly. The dog turns into a piece of furniture that sheds hair and fleas, and which people trip over on their way out the door. What would this dog think about the Five Freedoms?

How to have a happy dog

➤Is your dog losing out because it's been badly trained? With patience and time, you can cure most dogs of bad habits. In fact, you have a responsibility to the dog to do so. A dog that's seen as a nuisance will be an unhappy animal because it won't be a fully accepted member of its human pack. Here are some general guidelines for getting rid of bad habits.

1 Go to the library and find a book on dog behaviour so that you understand why dogs act the way they do.

2 If your dog is aggressive towards other dogs or towards people, ask your vet for help.

3 Choose one word that you'll give as a command every time your dog behaves badly. 'No' is a good choice because it's short and simple and works in many situations.

4 Be consistent. This isn't as easy as it sounds. It means that every time a bad habit occurs within your sight or hearing, you should correct your dog no matter what else is going on. And 'No' should always mean no.

5 Always reinforce the good behaviour you want with plenty of praise. Put some excitement into your voice and raise its pitch as you say something like, 'What a good dog!' If you lavish praise on your dog every time it does something you want, it will soon get the message and start trying to earn your praise again by repeating the behaviour that won the praise in the first place.

6 Try to avoid slaps to punish bad behaviour. If your dog does something really bad and you feel you absolutely must punish it, do it while the dog's misbehaving. If you punish it afterwards, the dog will have forgotten what it did and will only be confused by your behaviour.

7 Be patient. Some behaviour is instinctive and will take time to control.

8 Make sure you reward your dog only while it's doing the right thing. You'll confuse the dog if you reward it while it's still behaving badly. The dog will quite reasonably think that's the behaviour you want it to continue doing.

Is your dog a jumper?

➤A dog jumps up because it wants attention. The secret to training a jumper not to jump is to give it the attention it craves when it's sitting quietly. Each time the dog jumps up, gently knee it in the chest to unbalance it and give a stern command of 'Sit.' Lavish lots of attention on the dog only when it sits.

Is your dog a chewer?

➤Chewing is usually a problem with puppies who chew to make their gums feel better when they're teething. If you have a puppy that loves to chew, first remove all tempting objects that you don't want it to chew, and give it a rawhide or another chew toy. If an older dog has a chewing habit, extra exercise might help it sleep through more of the day, which leaves less (possibly unsupervised) time for it to wreak havoc on your valuables.

Does your dog refuse to come when called?

➤Find a piece of rope about 9 m (30 feet) long and tie it to your dog's collar. Allow the dog to wander off. When it's the full length of the rope away, call the dog and give the rope a tug. Put some fun into the way you call so that the dog has some incentive to come back to you and make sure you lavish it with praise when it finally does return (with the aid of a few *gentle* tugs on the rope). Whatever you do, never call your dog and then punish it. Would you come willingly to someone who punished you the last time you responded to their call?

QUIZ

Talking the talk

You don't need spoken language to understand cats and dogs, just an ability to read body language. Test your Doolittle skills in this silent quiz. Be careful. Sometimes there's more than one correct answer.

1. If your dog greets you at the door by bowing to you, with its bum in the air, it's saying:
a. Am I glad to see you!
b. I've got an awful itch, will you scratch it please?
c. Will you play with me?

2. Occasionally your pet cat touches your face with its paw. It's telling you that:
a. You've got bad breath.
b. You're a member of my family.
c. You'd look much better with whiskers.

3. When your dog wakes up in the morning, it often rolls onto its back so you can rub its tum. What's it saying?
a. I'll scratch yours if you'll scratch mine.
b. There's nothing like a good scratch to start the day.
c. You're top dog around here and I'll do anything you want.

4. If your cat yawns around you, you should yawn back or blink slowly. But what are both saying?
a. I can really relax around you.
b. You're the most boring creature on Earth.
c. I've got something stuck in a back tooth. Can you see it?

(Answers page 224)

EPILOGUE

> 'Animals are happy so long as they have health and enough to eat'.
> Bertrand Russell, **The Conquest of Happiness** (1930) Routledge, Bertrand Russell Peace Foundation

Years ago, when Bertrand Russell made that statement, the common belief was that animals had little or no awareness of themselves or the world around them. They didn't need visiting rights, designer stalls with a view, sunshine or exercise to be happy in captivity because they weren't aware that they were missing them. All they needed was to feel generally OK and enjoy a full belly on a regular basis.

Since then, opinion has changed. Not about amoebas, barnacles, earthworms or other simple animals (although no one is yet prepared to draw the line that separates aware from non-aware animals − a fact that offers little comfort to anyone who's ever swallowed a live oyster or plunged a live lobster into boiling water). But about the kinds of complex, 'higher' animals you've met in this book.

This change in opinion presents us with a new dilemma. If many animals are aware of themselves and of their own suffering, how can we continue to use them the way we do? How do we begin to square our new awareness of animals with what we do to them in zoos, factory farms, research laboratories and our own homes? It's difficult isn't it? As long as we hold on to the belief that animals aren't aware enough to suffer in captivity, we can turn a blind eye to what we do to them. But the moment we begin to see them as fellow, aware beings, who would choose not to suffer if given the opportunity (remember the choice made by the Tamworth Two?), they have the moral right not to suffer. And, because we're moral beings, we have the responsibility to make sure this happens.

Before you flip back through the pages of this book to decide whether you want to change any of the responses you made to the statements at the beginning of each section, there are a few more things you should consider. They might help you make up your mind.

Ask yourself who you should believe

➤People on both sides of the debate on animal rights sometimes fall into the trap of misinterpreting facts. When people feel passionately about something, it's understandable that they'll want to see confirmation of their beliefs in as many situations as possible and try to score points off the other side. So be wary of all or nothing claims. For instance, claims that medical research is entirely responsible for people living much longer today are as false as the claims that medical research did nothing to improve public health throughout the 20th century. Also, it's a mistake to place too much faith in the objectivity of scientific enquiry. All pharmaceutical companies have an interest in seeing animal research continue. Their profitability might well depend upon it. Zoos too have an interest in seeing captive breeding continue. Without the animals those breeding programmes generate, zoos would go out of business.

Haven't you noticed that it's always easier to criticize something than it is to do it right the first time? Animal rights supporters can pick an issue and sum it up neatly in a catchy slogan that tugs at the heartstrings, while scientists have to justify their work from within a rigid scientific framework that dictates every step they take. The result is that animal rights supporters often win the battle of words because they can take an all or nothing stance in the war against abuse of animals. And black and white issues are easier to grasp than complex issues that have to be qualified by cumbersome scientific explanations. But, as you've discovered, there are precious few black and white issues when it comes to how and why we use animals the way we do.

In short:

• Be wary of all or nothing/black or white claims by animal support groups.

• Always be ready to question the objectivity of any scientific findings produced by a group interested in maintaining the status quo.

Ask yourself if we are wrong to kill animals

►A quick recap shows that:

• We keep animals in zoos for our entertainment and sometimes our education. The best zoos also keep endangered animals captive so that they can breed them in captivity for possible release later into the wild. Zoos often kill off surplus animals from breeding programmes.

• We keep animals in factory farms so we can raise them for the smallest possible cost and with a minimum amount of work, then kill them so that we can eat them.

• We keep animals in research laboratories so we can test the safety of products or new treatments on them, then kill them to find out the results. Some research is done strictly for the sake of scientific knowledge.

►You'll notice that we kill animals in all three institutions. (We also assume the right to 'put down' our pets, and the RSPCA has to kill many thousands of unwanted pets annually.) You've already encountered the issue of whether it's right to kill animals, but this time approach it from the animal's point of view. One way of doing this is to ask whether animals are afraid of dying. Do they have a concept of death like we do? In other words, does seeing their companions suffer and die make them think about and fear their own death? If it does, raising them for the sole purpose of killing them, either to be eaten or to further the cause of medicine or scientific knowledge, is an act of cruelty.

Research has shown that primates, and maybe even elephants, have a concept of death similar to our own. It would appear, though, that the majority of animals do not. At least, that's what their behaviour suggests although we've already seen how easy it is to misinterpret animal behaviours. When sheep continue grazing after one of their companions is shot dead, even if the body is left lying around, we assume they're unaffected by the death, that they haven't been able to make the connection between the death of a companion and the possibility of harm and maybe even death coming to them. Of course, we can't be certain because we can't get inside a sheep's head and understand things as a sheep. But there's a very strong likelihood that if sheep show fear on their way to slaughter, it's probably not their own death they're fearing. It's having to walk up a scary ramp into an unknown space, and the unaccustomed, rough handling, harsh sounds and bright lights that make them anxious and afraid.

Where does that leave us?

►It would appear that many animals are aware of their own suffering but are not necessarily aware that one day they'll die, or that death is something to fear. There also seems to be plenty of evidence to suggest that captive animals suffer both physical and mental pain. Because we have the moral responsibility and the power to prevent animals suffering on our account, we should be looking for ways to make this happen. And we should be asking ourselves what moral rights animals have that we are willing to accept. They certainly don't need all the same rights that humans do. A dairy cow, for instance, doesn't feel her rights are violated because she's denied the opportunity to go to school. Yet if the same dairy cow could talk, she'd probably tell you her right to choose not to suffer is violated every day by humans who don't accept that what is right for them might also be right for other animals. Because the dairy cow – and all the other mammals and birds you've met in this book – have the capacity for suffering, the obvious conclusion is that they deserve the same consideration we currently reserve for ourselves.

Animal welfare researchers claim that we know how to give captive animals a good and satisfying life, just as we know how to give them a quick and painless death. Meanwhile, animal rights supporters, vegetarians and anti-vivisectionists claim that we should stop using animals as mere commodities and quit acting as if our own lives are the only ones of any value. But claims are one thing, action is another.

What can you do?

►The task is a daunting one, and it's doubtful that major change is going to happen overnight in the lives of captive animals. But there are several, very positive things you can do to help bring about gradual change in the way that institutions, industry and the government treat animals.

1 Use this book to check out the quality of your local zoo. If it fails the test ask your local council what can be done about it.

2 Support only responsible zoos that play an active role in conserving endangered species and demonstrate their concern for the happiness of their animals by improving the quality of their lives.

3 Demand that supermarkets subscribe to the RSPCA's Freedom Food campaign and refuse to buy meat, eggs and dairy produce from animals reared and slaughtered under inhumane conditions.

4 Whether you eat meat or not, campaign for more government support for farmers who choose to use more humane farming practices.

5 Take responsibility for your own health so that you reduce the risk of illness as you get older and so ease the burden on animals in laboratories.

6 Try not to buy products labelled 'new and/or improved' and ask yourself whether you really need as many new clothes, hair products, cosmetics, etc. as you normally might buy. Think hard about the true cost of our throw-away habits.

7 If you have a pet, make sure it enjoys all Five Freedoms.

8 Learn as much about animals as you can, and become a voice for them.

The decisions, and the actions, are all yours to make.

On 6 October 1997, Marks & Spencer Ltd. announced that in future they'd sell only free-range eggs. Their decision to ban battery eggs from all their British stores in 1997 and all their French stores in 1998 was brought about by public demand.

= HELPFUL =
CONTACTS AND
INFORMATION

Good stuff to read (written for teens)

James, Barbara. (1992) *The Young Person's Action Guide to Animal Rights* Virago Press, London
Informative, A-Z format that offers plenty of useful what-can-you-do suggestions.

Donnellan, Craig, (ed.) (1995) Do Animals Have Rights?
Independence Educational Publishers, Cambridge
A collection of articles giving various organizations' opposing points of view on animal research and animal sport.

Ganeri, Anita. (1997) *Animal Rights*
Hodder Children's Books, London
Brief overview of many animal rights issues, including the history behind the animal rights movement.

Other good stuff to read (adult books, but you'll find plenty here to grab your interest)

Bostock, Stephen St.C. (1993) *Zoos & Animal Rights: The ethics of keeping animals*
Routledge, London
Bostock makes a good attempt to come to terms with two opposing points of view - that animals have rights and that zoos are acceptable, even if he is talking about only a few enlightened zoos.

Clough, Caroline & Kew, Barry. (1993) The Animal Rights Welfare Book
Fourth Estate, London.
A useful guide with tons of facts, including information on all the major organizations and a terrific resource list.

Dawkins, Marian Stamp (1980) *Animal Suffering: the science of animal welfare*
Chapman and Hall, London
Dawkins, who pioneered research into what animals want, uses a scientific approach to discover how to tell whether an animal is suffering.

Dawkins, Marian Stamp (1993) *Through Your Eyes Only: the search for animal consciousness*
W.H. Freeman & Company Limited, Oxford
A fascinating exploration of what goes on inside animals' heads, with interesting anecdotes.

Eyton, A. (1991) *The Kind Food Guide*
Penguin Books, London
A fast, easy read that can help you make animal-friendly choices when it comes to food.

Gould, James L. and Gould, Carol Grant (1994) *The Animal Mind*
Scientific American Library, New York
The things that scientists have to do to figure out whether animals act on instinct or think about what they're doing are definitely worth reading.

Harrison, Ruth (1964) *Animal Machines*
This landmark book on the plight of animals in factory farms led directly to the establishment of the government's Brambell Committee and the Farm Animal Welfare Council.

Ironmonger, John (1992) *The Good Zoo Guide*
HarperCollins Publishers, London
Check out how Ironmonger rates some of the country's best zoos after you've rated your local zoo.

Johnson, A. (1991) *Factory Farming*
Basil Blackwell Ltd., Oxford
Everything you wanted to know (or perhaps wish you
didn't have to know) about the welfare of animals in
factory farms and slaughter houses.

Masson, Jeffrey Moussaieff and McCarthy, Susan (1995)
When Elephants Weep: the emotional lives of animals
Delacorte Press, New York
Easy to read and guaranteed to change the way you think
about animals.

Singer, Peter (1995 ed.) *Animal Liberation*
Pimlico, London
The 1975 edition of this landmark book was once hailed
as the 'bible' of the animal rights movement.

Tudge, Colin (1991) *Last Animals at the Zoo*
Hutchinson Radius, London
A behind-the-scenes peek at zoo conservation work.
Offers an excellent defence of captive breeding.

The Zoo Inquiry (1994), a report published jointly by the
World Society for the Protection of Animals and
the Born Free Foundation.
Sparked an avalanche of articles and debates with its
claim that zoos do little to conserve endangered animals.

Webster, J. (1994) *Animal Welfare: a cool eye towards Eden*
Blackwell Science Ltd., Oxford
Webster is a thoughtful animal welfare researcher, and
his book looks at the needs of farm and laboratory
animals as well as wild animals and pets and what they
should expect from us.

Some useful addresses to contact for further information

I Animals in zoos

International Zoo News
80 Cleveland Road
Chichester
West Sussex PO19 2FH
(Ask for free sample copy.)

The Born Free Foundation (includes Zoo Check)
Cherry Tree Cottage
Anstie Lane
Coldharbour, Dorking
Surrey RH5THA
Telephone: 01306 712 091
Fax: 01306 713 350

World Society for the Protection of Animals
2 Langley Lane
London SW8 ITJ
Telephone: 0171 793 0540
Fax: 0171 793 0208

The Association of British Wild Animal Keepers
c/o John Partridge
2A Northcote Road
Clifton, Bristol BS8 3HB
(Publishes *Ratel*, which gives a behind-the-scenes look at zoo keeping. Ask for back issue list.)

The Federation of Zoological Gardens of Great Britain and Ireland suggests contacting the following

Members for specific information about British Zoos:

1. London Zoo, Zoological Gardens, Regent's Park,
London, NW1 4RY
Telephone 0171 722 3333
2. Chester Zoo, Zoological Gardens, Upton-by-Chester,
CH2 1LH
Telephone 01244 380280
3. Edinburgh Zoo, Scottish National Zoological Park,
Murrayfield, Edinburgh EH12 6TS
Telephone 0131 334 9171
4. Bristol Zoo Gardens, Clifton, Bristol BS8 3HA
Telephone 0117 970 6176
5. Whipsnade Wild Animal Park, Nr. Dunstable, Beds.
LU6 2LF
Telephone 0990 200123
6. Twycross Zoo Park, Norton-juxta-Twycross,
Atherstone, Warwicks. CV9 3PX
Telephone 01827 880250
7. Paignton Zoo, Totnes Road, Paignton, Devon TQ4 7ED
Telephone 01803 557479
(*The Good Zoo Guide*, see page 214, lists many more.)

2 Animals in factory farms

Advocates for Animals
10 Queensferry Street
Edinburgh EH2 4PG

Agricultural & Food Research Council
Institute of Animal Physiology
Brabraham Hall
Brabraham
Cambridgeshire CB2 4AT

Animal Aid
The Old Chapel
Bradford Street
Tonbridge
Kent TN9 1AW
(http://www.envirolink.org/ARRS/AAid)

Compassion In World Farming Trust
5A Charles Street
Petersfield
Hants GU32 3EH
(http://www.ibmpcug.co.uk/-ciwf/)

Council for Justice to Animals & Humane Slaughter
Association
34 Blanche Lane
South Mimms
Potters Bar
Hertfordshire ENB6 3PA

Free Range Egg Association
37 Tanza Road
London NW3 2UA

Ministry of Agriculture
Information Division
Whitehall Place (West Branch)
London SW1A 2HH
0171 238 6001

The Farm Animal Welfare Council
Block B
Government Buildings
Hook Rise South

Tolworth
Surbiton
Surrey KT6 7NF
(the government's watchdog on welfare)

The Soil Association
86 Colston Street
Bristol BS1 5BB
(e-mail: soilassoc@gn.apc.org)

The Vegan Society
Donald Watson House
7 Battle Road
St. Leonards-on-Sea
East Sussex TN37 7AA

3 Animals in research laboratories

These organizations support the responsible use of
animals in medical research.

Animals in Medicines Research
Information Centre
12 Whitehall
London SW1A 2DY

Biomedical Research Education Trust
Suite 501
International House
223 Regent Street
London W1R 8QD

Research for Health Charities Group
P.O. Box 1417
Shepton Mallet
Somerset BA4 4YZ

RDS: Understanding Animal Research in Medicine
58 Great Marlborough Street
London W1V 1DD

Seriously Ill for Medical Research
P.O. Box 504
Dunstable
Beds LU6 2LU

These organizations are concerned with the welfare of research animals:

Dr Hadwen Trust for Humane Research
22 Bancroft, Hitchin
Hertfordshire SG5 1JW

Fund for the Replacement of Animals in Medical Research
Russell & Burch House
96–98 North Sherwood Street
Nottingham NG1 4EE

Humane Research Trust
Brook House
29 Bramhall Lane South
Bramhall
Cheshire SK7 2DN

Royal Society for the Prevention of Cruelty to Animals
Causeway
Horsham
West Sussex RH12 1HG

Universities Federation for Animal Welfare
8 Hamilton Close
South Mimms
Potters Bar
Herts EN6 3QD

These organizations are concerned with animal rights:

Animal Aid
The Old Chapel
Bradford Street
Tonbridge
Kent TN9 1AW

British Union for the Abolition of Vivisection
16a Crane Grove
London N7 8LB

National Anti-Vivisection Society
261 Goldhawk Road
London W12 9PE

4 This organization represents cosmetic companies

Cosmetic Toiletry and Perfumery Association
Josaron House
5-7 John Princes Street
London W1M 9HD

5 This organization is against animal testing of cosmetics

Body Shop International
Education Dept.
Watersmead
Littlehampton
West Sussex BN17 6LS

Most organizations listed will send you free material if you write to them and include an A3 stamped, self-addressed envelope.

Answers to Would you know an endangered animal if you met one? page 56

Panda **** Lion **** Tiger **** Rhinoceros****
Leopard*** Polar bear* Gorilla*** Orangutan****
Chimpanzee*** Elephant**** Giraffe* Zebra***

Answers to True or false?, page 111

1 – True – Supermarkets control the quantity and quality of the foods they buy. For instance, livestock must
be of a certain size and fat content, carrots must be straight, apples must be unblemished.

2 – True – This doesn't include the £1275 million spent previously on water treatment equipment.

3 – True – Soil erosion is the culprit and, while there are a number of causes of soil erosion, many of them are linked with our over-consumption of animal products. An estimated 40 percent of arable land in England and
Wales is now one quarter less productive thanks to erosion from intensive farming practices.

4 – True – Britain's 850 registered organic farmers cannot keep up with the demand for their products. One
way you can help farmers convert to organic methods and so increase the supply is to ask the Minister of
Agriculture, Fisheries and Food for better financial help for farmers under the government's Organic Aid
Scheme.

5 – True – You can help this prediction come true by buying and demanding more organic produce.

6 – True – Each year, cattle alone consume enough food to satisfy the calorie needs of almost double the
human population.

7 – True – When factory farmed animals are denied straw bedding, their excrement turns into a semi-liquid

slurry, which is stored in lagoons. Often this slurry, which is much more polluting than human sewage, seeps out of the lagoons and finds its way into the water system.
8 – True – Many farmers are still critical of the intensive farming methods they have to adopt. (The intensive farming lobby is much bigger than just the farmers. It includes large corporations that supply feed, equipment, machinery and chemicals, and also research workers.)

Answer to A brain scrambler, pages 160-161

The hidden question by Jeremy Bentham is: 'The question is not, Can they reason? Can they talk? But can they suffer?'

Answers to Talking the talk, page 202

1-a and c; 2-b, 3-c, 4-a